Sticks & Stones & Ice Cream Cones

Sticks & Stones & Ice Cream Cones

The Craft Book for Children

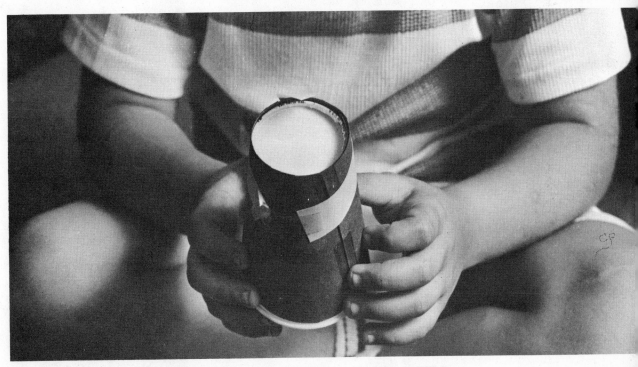

by PHYLLIS FIAROTTA with NOEL FIAROTTA

 WORKMAN PUBLISHING COMPANY
New York

ISBN:
  Cloth—0-911104-29-1
  Paper—0-911104-30-5

First printing October 1973
Second printing December 1973
Third printing April 1974

Workman Publishing Company, Inc.
231 East 51st Street
New York, New York 10022

Manufactured in the United States of America

Contributing editor: Noel Fiarotta
Illustrations: Phyllis Fiarotta
Cover: Paul Hanson
Photographs: Barbara and Justin Kerr

To Father, whom I still call Daddy, an unconventional
genius with a quiet, loving heart

Table of Contents

Foreword to parents

The return to craftwork is on. How-to-make-it items are displayed everywhere you look, and men and women alike discover the pleasure of making quality products themselves. Children especially love craftwork, and should at last be given the chance to create and use handmade games, toys, and things of beauty. *Sticks & Stones & Ice Cream Cones* provides the opportunity. It is the first book of its kind to offer youngsters a full range of craft projects on their own level; to help them explore completely all craft techniques.

This book belongs to the younger generation. It is written for children to understand. All specific measurements (inches and feet) are omitted, leaving the total creative process to the young craft designer. For easier construction, many of the projects are illustrated in exact project-sized patterns. No guesswork is needed.

Some crafts will appeal to your children, others will not. Don't force them, just for creativity's sake, to make something they won't use. Let them choose the objects they would like to construct. They will automatically select the things most appropriate to their age group. Your children know themselves very well and what it is that they most enjoy making.

The adult plays an important part in the construction process. Read through this book before you hand it over to your children. Look at all of the craft items and see how the instructions are written. **You will notice the symbol ** in front of a direction. This means that potentially dangerous household equipment is called for, or that the execution of the step so marked may be too difficult for a child.** It is advisable for you to supervise this activity. Keep in mind your children's physical abilities and limitations. If you feel they cannot perform a particular task, you will have to do it for them. Allow youngsters to feel, however, that they are the ones creating the objects, even though it is you who have just bored a hole in a piece of wood or cut a piece of string.

Every craft item in this book has three parts: the drawing, the instructions, and a list of craft materials. Children should be encouraged to read through the instructions several times before they begin, and to study the drawings carefully. You will provide them with the necessary craft supplies. Almost all materials can be bought in a stationery or art supply store, or at the stationery counter of department stores. Other needed items will be found in your kitchen or in the family tool box. One of the greatest pluses of the craft boom is that it recycles paper and metal products. Coffee cans, oatmeal boxes, and shirt cardboard are just a few of the many items that can be reused. Save all throwaways for future craft use.

It is now time to present this book to its rightful owners, your children. There are hours of fun and creativity—of toy, craft and game making—between its covers. And if, by chance, you find yourself the recipient of one of the beautiful, handmade craft objects, consider yourself lucky indeed. Your reward is a gift from the heart—your child's special sense of accomplishment.

Just for you

This is *your* craft book. It contains many interesting things for you to make all by yourself. Crafts like macrame and candle making; all kinds of toys and games; even a complete puppet show for you to design, produce and perform. There are toys to make from other lands, things which fly, things to grow. Holiday decorations, party favors—beautiful gifts for special people . . .

Look through the book and see all the great things you can do. Decide which item you would like to make first. It is very important that you read all directions—not just once, but several times before you begin. If there is something you don't understand, have someone explain it to you. It is important to study the drawings well, too. You will be better able to understand the directions if you see how a craft is put together. Your mom and dad will buy and help you find all the materials you'll need for the projects you choose. If you have difficulty cutting, threading, sewing or *anything*, ask for a helping hand. Once you learn the way to handle tools and materials, the construction of the items will be easier.

Now choose the items that you would like to have or make the most. Take your time with the projects and do the best job you can. If something does not turn out to be as perfect as you would like it, don't worry. Your individuality will add a personal touch to every craft you make. Besides, there's always more to try, again and again. Think of this book as a chocolate layer cake: one slice is never enough.

All about the things you need

PAPER

• **White drawing paper** is important in craft projects as well as for drawing. Drawing paper is heavy, smooth paper that comes in pads or packages.

• **Colored construction paper** is heavy paper that comes in many wonderful colors. The sheets are sold in packages, and many paper sizes are available. Try to pick the correct size for the craft you will be making. Save all large scraps in a box or bag. You never know when you might need a little bit of color.

• **Tracing paper** is very important for many of your craft projects. It is very light, transparent paper. When it is placed on a drawing, you can see the drawing through it. Tracing paper comes in pads.

• **Typewriter paper** is a white paper that is lighter than white drawing paper but heavier than tracing paper. You can see a drawing under it. It comes in packaged sheets.

• **Cardboard** is very heavy paper. You can find it backing shirts which come from the laundry or in packages of new clothes. Other boxes found around the house—like shoe and hat boxes—are made of it. Cardboard may also be bought in art supply stores. Save all pieces of cardboard you find in your home.

GLUES AND PASTES

• **Liquid white glue** comes in plastic bottles with pointed caps. This glue makes a strong bond when it dries and is used, therefore, for hard-to-glue crafts.

• **Liquid brown glue,** or mucilage, comes in a bottle with a rubber cap that is used for spreading. It is a light adhesive.

• **Paper paste** is a white, thick adhesive. It comes usually in a jar, and has a plastic spreader. Paper paste is best for sticking paper to paper.

• **Wallpaper paste** is a powder paste that you mix with water. Although it is used in putting up wallpaper, we will use it for making some of the crafts.

COLORINGS

• **Poster paints** are paints that can be removed from your hands with water. They come in many colors and are sold in jars.

• **Watercolor paints** are little tablets of hard color that must be daubed with a wet brush to use. The paints come in a tin which has at least six colors in it.

• **Crayons** are colored wax sticks that are used for drawing.

• **Colored felt-tipped markers** are tubes or "pencils" of enclosed watercolor with a felt coloring tip. You draw with markers as you would with crayons.

• **Indelible felt-tipped markers** are special markers that use unremovable or unwashable "inks" for coloring. Use indelible felt markers only for the crafts that ask for them specifically.

BRUSHES

• **A watercolor brush** is a small brush that is used for fine drawing, like painting pictures of faces.

• **Paintbrushes** are larger. They are used to paint large surface areas, like the sides of a box.

FABRIC

• **Felt** is a strong, heavy fabric that comes in many colors. It is sold in small squares. It can be glued to a surface with liquid white glue.

• **Scrap fabric** is odds and ends of cloth that your mom saves from her sewing projects. You can also cut up old clothes for scrap fabric.

How to trace patterns from this book

HOW TO TRACE PATTERNS FROM THIS BOOK

There are many projects in this book you make with your imagination. All it takes is some scissors and paper and—puff—you have a beautiful craft. There are other things for which you will need a little more than just your imagination. For these crafts you will need to make a pattern.

The patterns in this book are drawn with a heavier line than the other illustrations. Instructions about patterns will always be given along with the directions on making the craft.

TO TRACE A PATTERN

1. Place a sheet of tracing paper over the page that has the pattern you wish to trace, Fig. a.
2. Follow the outline of the pattern with a soft pencil on the tracing paper. Do not press hard or you will see pencil marks on the page.
3. After you have traced the pattern on tracing paper, cut it out with your scissors, Fig. b.

(Never cut any pattern out of your book.)
4. Put the new cutout pattern on the paper you wish to use, Fig. c.
5. With a pencil, trace around the edge of the cutout pattern, Fig. c.
6. Remove the cutout pattern and cut out the new drawing from the paper. Now you are ready to continue with your project, Figs. d and e.

TO TRACE A PATTERN WITH A PENCIL RUBBING

Another way of tracing from this book is with a pencil rubbing. With this method, you do not have to cut out the pattern from the tracing paper.

1. Place a sheet of tracing paper over the page that has the pattern you wish to trace.
2. Follow the outline of the pattern with a soft pencil, Fig. a.
3. After you have traced the pattern from the book, turn the tracing paper over, and rub along the back of the tracing outline with the

side of the pencil lead. Make sure the back-and-forth scribbling covers all of the pattern outline, Fig. f.

4. Place the tracing over the paper you wish to use, scribbled side down, Fig. g.

5. Draw over the lines of the original tracing with a pencil. Press hard on the line as you draw. The rubbing will act like carbon paper.

6. Lift up the tracing paper.

7. The lead that you scribbled on the back of the tracing paper will have come off on the paper where you drew with your pencil, Fig. h.

8. Cut out the drawing from the paper and continue with your project.

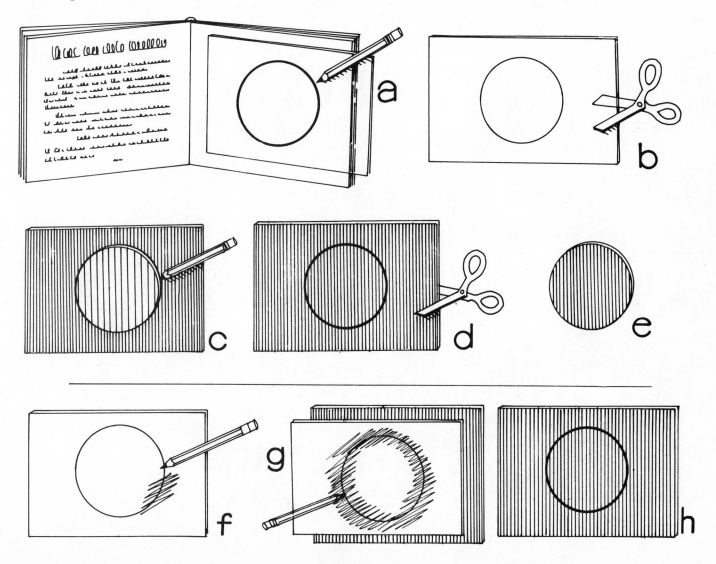

Flying
through the air
with the
greatest of ease

Flying through the air with the greatest of ease

For a second or two, the man on the flying trapeze soars gracefully through the air. He flies over his audience without wings of feather or tail of steel, caught—just in time—in the mighty hands of his partner. After one good swing he rockets upward again, returning in triumph to his lofty perch. Once his feet are safely on the platform, the audience applauds his marvelous flying stunts.

Have you ever tried to fly? No doubt you had a few problems. Only birds, bats, bees, butterflies, and other flying insects can move freely through the air. Of course, there are machines that fly—things like jets, gliders, helicopters, and rockets. With these, man has managed to get closer and closer to the sun, moon, and stars. Wouldn't it be great if you could do that anytime you wanted?

In this chapter you almost can. You can bring the sky and some of its wonders right into your very own bedroom. The toys included here will let you take an imaginary trip to the moon, make your very own star, decorate your ceiling with all kinds of flying creatures. You may not really be the man on the flying trapeze, but you can feel something like the way he feels, just by creating the objects which follow.

Spinning Star Wheels

"Twinkle, twinkle little star, how I wonder what you are . . ." These are very familiar words to you. Have you ever looked at a cloudless evening sky and seen the stars twinkling? They don't, really. Because stars are so far away, their light has to travel millions and millions of miles before you can see it. The light shines through space dust and other objects surrounding the earth, and this is what makes them seem to twinkle.

Maybe stars spin. Since you cannot take a rocket ship into space to find out for yourself, you'll have to use your imagination. Bring a piece of the sky into your hands. Create a special star. This one will catch the wind and whirl in dizzy circles, like a crazy earth spinning around the sun. If the air is still, hold the wheel in your hand and twirl yourself in circles. You will enjoy seeing your star go round and round.

Things You Need

1 square piece of colored construction paper
scissors
1 nail with a large head
1 new pencil
stick-on gold stars
1 bead

Let's Begin

1. Start with a square piece of construction paper; you choose the color. Be sure all sides are of equal size.
2. Draw a line from corner to corner. This forms an X on the paper, Fig. a.
3. Cut along these lines up to O, as shown in Fig. a. Do not cut all the way to the center.
4. Number the corners as shown: 1, 2, 3, 4.
5. Bring corner 1 to the center, Fig. b.
6. Bring corner 2 over corner 1, Fig. c.
7. Bring corner 3 over corner 2.
8. Bring corner 4 over corner 3.
9. Ask Dad or Mom for a long nail with a large head. Push the nail through the four points and all the way through the center of the star wheel.
**10. Hammer the nail through the eraser of a new pencil.
11. Glue a bead over the point of the nail that came through the other side of the eraser.
12. Stick gold stars onto the wheel.
13. Hold star to the wind or whirl around.

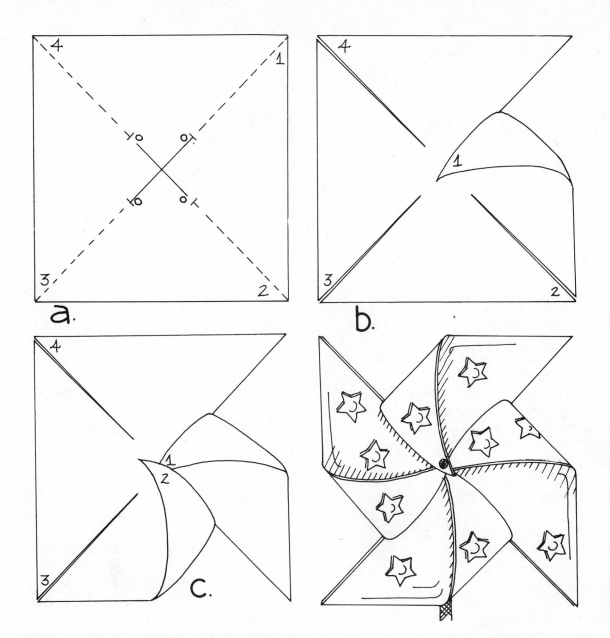

a.

b.

C.

Gliding Paper Airplanes

A glider rides the rising air currents without the roar of a turning propeller. The only sound that can be heard is the wind blowing over the wings of the plane. You've probably never been in a gliding airplane, but you can build your very own. All it takes is a piece of paper, a paper clip, and a little energy you supply to make this aircraft fly.

If you really enjoy "piloting" your first paper airplane, make dozens of them. You might be the captain of your own air force, or the owner of a flying school. You and your friends can have hours of fun racing planes, seeing how high they can fly, competing to design the best-looking models.

Things You Need

1 sheet of typewriter paper

1 paper clip
crayons or colored felt-tipped markers

Let's Begin

1. Fold a sheet of paper in half along the long side, Fig. a.
2. Keep the folded side on the bottom. Corner X (Fig. a.) is folded over to lie on the folded side, Fig. b.
3. Do the same with the other corner.
4. Corner Z (Fig. c.) is then folded over to lie flat on the folded bottom. This will cover Corner X, Fig. a.
5. Do the same with the other corner.
6. You now have two wing flaps, Fig. e. Fold these on each side of the plane in such a way that Y is lower than the bottom folded side, Fig. f.
7. Slip a paper clip near the front point.
8. Draw designs with crayons or markers.

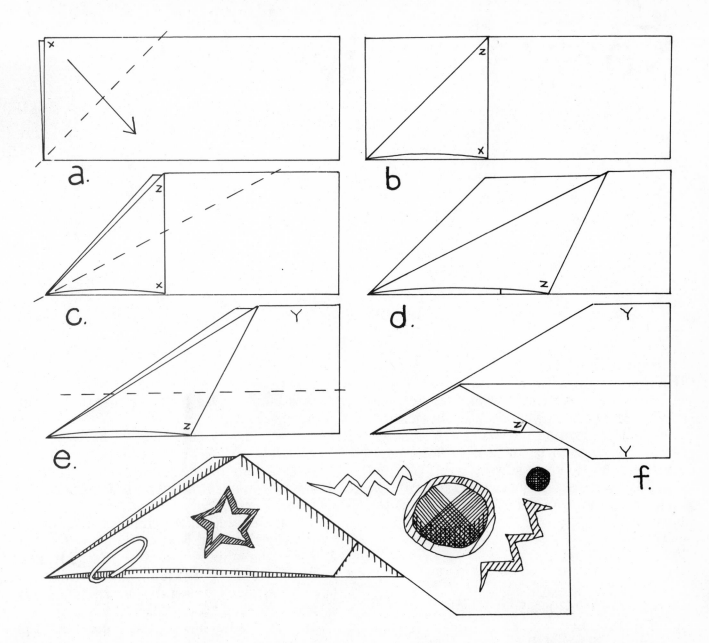

a.

b.

c.

d.

e.

f.

Noisy Sun Rattlers

"Happy New Year!" "No more school!" "Happy birthday!"

There are many times when you are very happy. So what do you do? Celebrate. And what is a celebration without a lot of noise? You don't want to be too noisy, but you do want everyone to know how you feel. Why not do it with these out-of-space sun rattlers? The noise from your sun rattlers will shake up a merry beat.

Things You Need

2 deep paper plates
1 handful of dried beans
liquid white glue
crayons or colored felt-tipped markers

Let's Begin

1. Ask Mom or Dad for two paper plates with a raised rim.
2. Draw a happy sun face on the bottom or underside of each plate. Use crayons or colored felt-tipped markers.
3. Place a handful of dried beans inside one plate, Fig. a.
4. Put white glue on the rim of the plate containing the dried beans.
5. Place the empty plate over the plate that has the white glue around the rim.
6. Let the glued plates dry overnight. From the side, the rattler will look like Fig. b.
7. Hold in your hands and shake for fun noises.

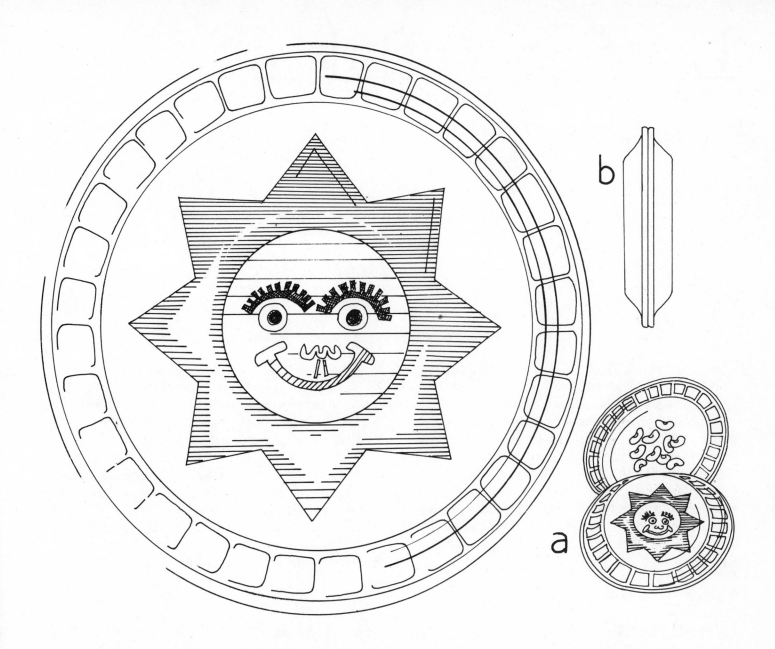

b

a

Lacy Snowflakes

It has been said that no two snowflakes look the same. Can this really be true? Since nobody can see all of the snowflakes during a snowstorm, there might just be twins. When it snows, what fun it is to catch snowflakes softly on your glove or coat. You could look at them for hours. Each one is so beautiful and appears unlike any other—maybe it *is* true that no two snowflakes look alike.

Whether you live where there is too much snow or where snow never comes, you'll want a blizzard in your bedroom. Make as many Lacy Snowflakes as it'll take, and hang them from your ceiling, place them around your mirror, or just save them for holiday decoration. These are very special snowflakes. No matter how warm your room is, they'll never melt.

Things You Need

4 drinking straws
1 large paper doily
liquid white glue
stapler
tape
string

Let's Begin

1. Take two straws and cross them, Fig. a. Now tape them together where they meet.
2. Do the same with the other two straws.
3. Place the two crosses on top of each other, Fig. b.
4. Staple the two crosses together in the center. (You may tape them together if you'd rather.)
5. Cut out the round shapes from a paper doily.
6. Glue a round doily shape to the end of a straw, Fig. c.
7. Cover each straw end with a round doily shape.
8. When you are finished put a piece of string through one of the holes of the doily rounds and hang.

a

b

c

Cardboard Butterfly Printer

Everyone likes to watch a butterfly dance gracefully about the flowers and trees. As it flutters around, it looks as if the sky has a flower flying in it. Butterflies are very pretty because they are so colorful, but don't forget what it takes for them to get that way. They are caterpillars when they are first born. A caterpillar lives in large trees, eats plenty of green leaves, then spins a silky cocoon. It sleeps all winter in that cocoon and, come spring, finally emerges—a beautiful butterfly.

You don't have to wait until spring to see a butterfly. You don't even have to find a caterpillar. With a piece of cardboard and a pair of scissors you can make a butterfly printer. Hundreds of colorful butterflies can be yours— all you have to do is print them on paper, walls, book covers, or anywhere you want a little beauty for your own.

Things You Need

1 sheet of tracing paper
liquid white glue
watercolor brush
drawing paper
scissors
1 piece of cardboard
poster paint
pencil
crayons
colored felt-tipped markers

Let's Begin

1. Trace the butterflies from the book onto the tracing paper.
2. Cut out the tracings, and using them as patterns, trace shapes onto cardboard.
3. Cut out the cardboard butterflies and glue each to other pieces of cardboard with liquid white glue. The backing cardboard pieces should be larger than the butterfly shapes, Fig. a. Let the glued butterflies dry.
4. Paint a thin layer of poster paint over a butterfly shape only. Don't let the paint dry.
5. Print a butterfly immediately by turning the cardboard upside down and pressing the printer onto a piece of paper.
6. Lift the printer off the piece of paper.
7. Let the paint dry.
8. Add butterfly designs to print with crayons, felt-tipped markers, or poster paints.

a

Soaring Rocket Ship

How would you like to be an astronaut? You may be too young to fly a real rocket ship, but why not build your own? Just think, you can have a blast-off right in your own home. Travel your house, making each room a different star or planet. You're in control. Land on a meteor (that looks suspiciously like an armchair) or hop about the moon craters. When your exciting trip is over, lay your rocket safely in your room and think about tomorrow's fantastic journey. What about visiting your neighbor's galaxy next door?

Things You Need

1 cardboard tube from paper towels
poster paints
1 sheet of tracing paper
colored construction paper
scissors
tape
liquid white glue
paint brush
pencil

Let's Begin

1. You will need a cardboard tube, the kind found inside a roll of paper towels, for the body or fuselage of the rocket.
2. Get the tube and paint it a good rocket color with poster paints.
3. Trace Shapes a, b, and c from the book onto tracing paper.
4. Cut out the tracings and, using them as patterns, trace shapes onto construction paper. Make one tracing of Shape a, four of Shape b, and two of Shape c. Use different colored construction paper for each kind of shape.
5. Cut all shapes out of construction paper.
6. The nosecone is Shape a. To form it, keep point x (see book) on top as you roll paper so that corner Y meets Z. Tape the nosecone together, Fig. a.
7. The tail of the rocket is made from the four Shape b's. Fold each shape along the dotted line as shown in Fig. b.
8. The blasting flames of the rocket are made from the two Shape c's. Cut slits along the bottom of each shape, see dotted lines in Fig. c.
9. Attach all of the rocket parts to the fuselage with liquid white glue as follows:
10. Glue the nosecone over the top of the tube.
11. Glue the four tails on the bottom of the tube. Be sure they are equally spaced.
12. Glue the two flames inside the bottom of the tube.
13. Add a paper door and round windows.

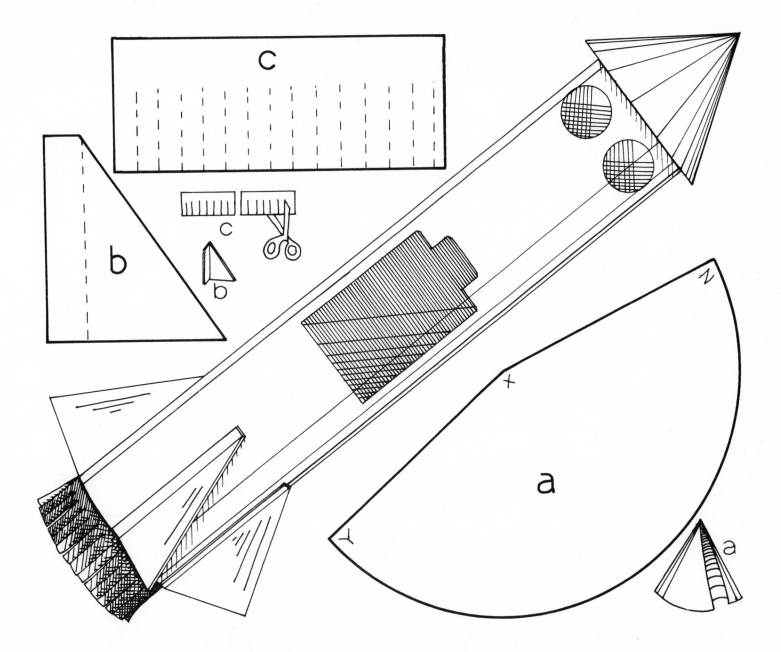

Twirling Copters

A toy helicopter won't fly. You have to move it along the ground. A Twirling Copter will go high into the sky. It is very simple to make and what fun you will have when you throw it into the air. The exciting part is watching it spin to the ground. The two blades look like they are playing a game of tag with each other. When the Twirling Copter lands, it is time for you to toss it into the sky again.

Things You Need

1 strip of paper
1 paper clip

Let's Begin

1. Cut out a long, narrow strip of paper, or trace the strip from the book.
2. Fold the strip in half, Fig. a.
3. Fold one top end of the folded strip down so that it points to the right, Fig. b.
4. Turn the paper over, Fig. c.
5. Fold the other top end of the folded strip of paper just as you did before, Fig. d.
6. Place a paper clip over the bottom folded part of the copter, Fig. d.
7. Throw it high into the air.

a   b   c   d

Whirling Birds

"A bird in the hand is worth two in the bush." Have you ever heard these words? What they mean is to be happy with what you have for the meantime. Now you'll have a "bird in the hand" for your very own. It won't fly away because it is attached to a stick. With your help, this feathered friend will do all kinds of tricks for you.

Things You Need

1 Twirling Copter (see page 36)
1 sheet of tracing paper
1 piece of cardboard
colored construction paper
liquid white glue or paper paste
1 new pencil
paper punch or sharp pencil
poster paints
1 straight pin
crayons or colored felt-tipped markers
length of yarn
1 cork

Let's Begin

1. Trace the bird, Shape a, from the book onto tracing paper.
2. Cut out the tracing and, using it as a pattern, trace the shape onto a piece of cardboard.
3. Cut out the cardboard bird.
4. Make a hole near the bird's beak with a paper punch or the point of a sharp pencil.
5. Paint the bird with poster paint.
6. Trace the bird's wing, Shape b, from the book onto tracing paper.
7. Cut out the tracing and, using it as a pattern, trace two wing shapes onto construction paper. Cut these out.
8. Put liquid white glue or paper paste on the rounded part of the wing.
9. Glue a wing onto each side of the bird.
10. Use crayons, colored felt-tipped markers, or paint to draw feathers on the wings and body.
**11. Have Mom or Dad cut a slit on the wide end of a cork from a bottle, Fig. c.
12. The tail is a Twirling Copter. It is attached to the bottom of the cork.
**13. To attach the tail, push a straight pin through the inside of the tail and into the cork. Don't push the pin in all the way, Fig. c.
14. Push the tail end of the bird into the slit in the cork.
15. Tie and knot a length of yarn through the hole on the bird's beak. Tie the other end of the yarn to a pencil.
16. Whirl the bird over your head.

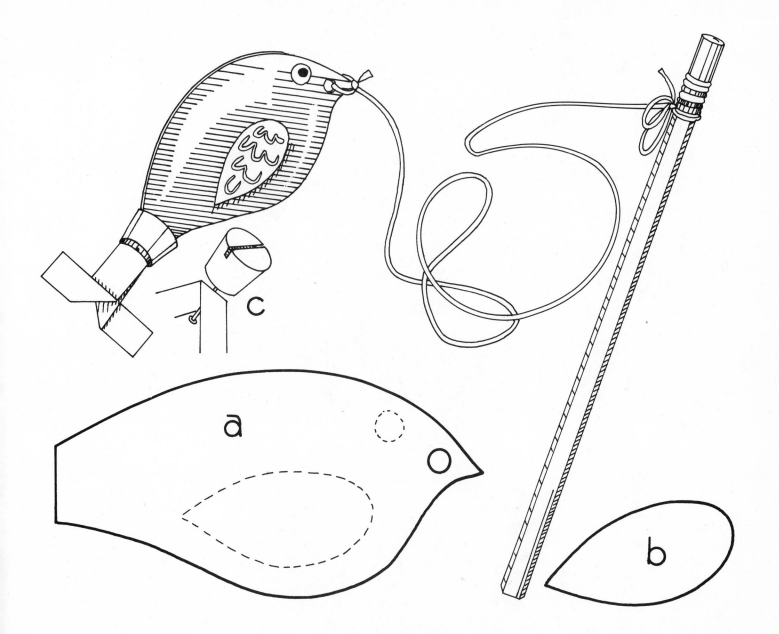

"The owl
and the pussycat
went to sea"

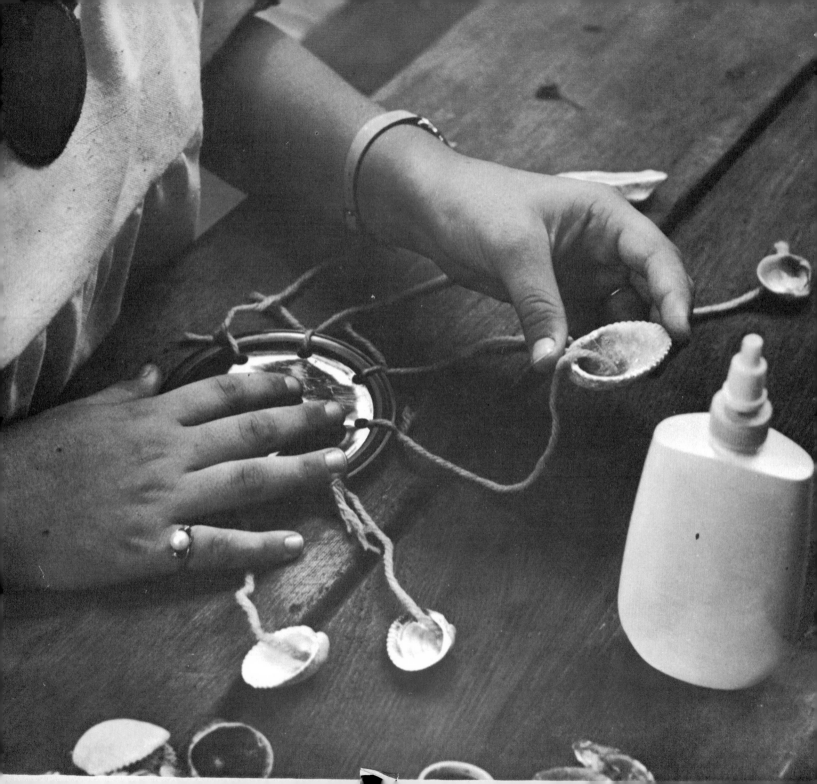

"The owl and the pussycat went to sea"

It was a long journey for the two weary travelers. The owl and the pussycat had set sail in search of a wedding ring. Since airplanes, cars, buses, and trains had not yet been invented, they traveled by boat. Riding on top of the blue ocean, the little craft with its crew of two finally reached land. When the ring was found—bought from a piggy for a shilling—the animals could at last be married and dance "by the light of the moon."

Have you every traveled the ocean in a boat, or merely looked at it? Standing by the shore, the sea is like a blue carpet being pulled by the beach. It is actually a gigantic home for millions of sea creatures. They have lived there longer than any other animals have lived on earth anywhere. In fact, the first land animal was probably some kind of fish that was ready to jump out of the ocean and check out the shore. He liked it so much that he dove back and told all his friends about the new dry world. After hundreds of millions of years, that fish's descendants evolved into all different types of land creatures. People today think that all creatures on earth came originally from the sea. Do you like that idea?

The next time you go to a beach, think about all this. Look down into the water and you will see some of the animals that make the ocean their home. Many of them, as you know, leave their shells behind on shore. Gather a bagful, and then see what beautiful "sea things" you can make in this chapter.

"Going Fishing" Game

"You should have seen the one that got away!"

Many fishermen say these words after a day of fishing. If this is true, there must be many big fish in the lakes, streams, and oceans. Big fish *are* hard to catch. They seem to be a little more careful than the smaller ones.

Big or small, it's hard to land a fish at home. But you can make a "Going Fishing" Game to play whenever you like with your friends. With it, there should be no reason why you can't catch your limit of fish—you might even be the best fisherman in your home!

Things You Need

1 sheet of tracing paper
cardboard
pencil
poster paints
watercolor brush
plastic shower-curtain hook
scissors
length of yarn
1 new pencil
1 gift box (shirt size)

Let's Begin

1. Trace the fish shape from the book onto tracing paper.
2. Cut out the tracing and, using it as a pattern, trace six fish shapes onto a piece of cardboard. Cut out the cardboard fish.
**3. Cut out or punch the large hole in the top of each fish.
4. Paint and decorate each fish.
5. Turn the gift box upside down.
6. Paint the box with green poster paint.
**7. Cut two rows of slits. Each row should have three slits equally spaced, see illustration.
8. Put one fish into each slit.
9. Tie a plastic shower-curtain hook on one end of a length of yarn.
10. Tie and knot the other end of the string around the top of a new pencil.
11. Try to fish by catching the plastic hook in the top hole of the fish. Pull the fish out of the box.

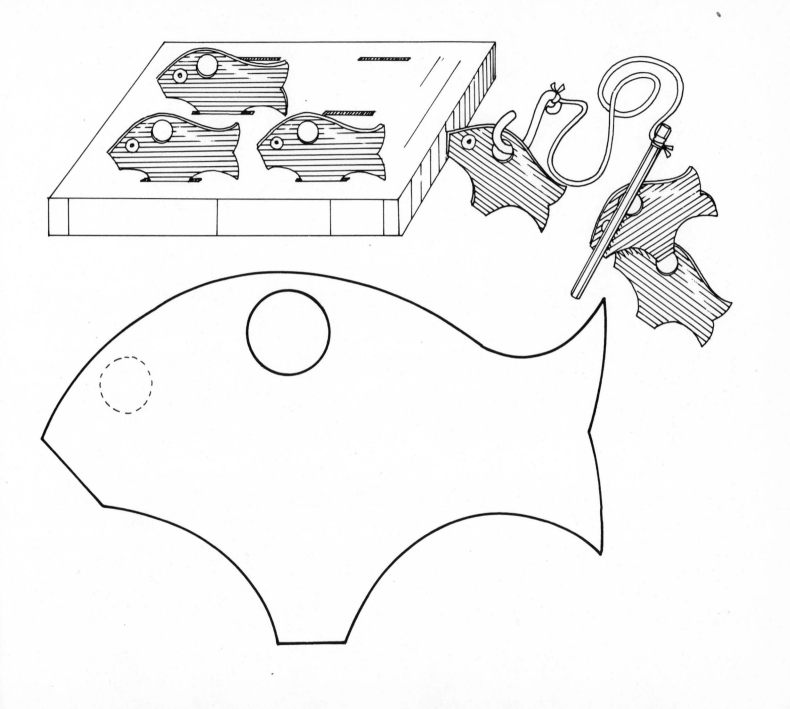

Tinkling Shell Wind Chime

If you are lucky enough to live near the ocean, you know how much fun it is to collect seashells. Hold the larger ones to your ear. You should hear a sound like the ocean's roaring waves.

There are many things you can make with seashells. For this craft idea you'll need at least eight pretty specimens. They should all be fairly small, but they needn't all look alike! The Tinkling Shell Wind Chime will make a lovely sound when the wind blows through it.

Things You Need

8 seashells (available, away from the beach, at craft supply stores)
1 plastic coffee-can lid
knitting yarn
liquid white glue
sharp pencil or paper punch

Let's Begin

1. Glue each shell to the end of a short piece of yarn. Use liquid white glue.
2. Dry overnight.
3. Punch eight holes equally spaced on the top of a plastic coffee-can lid. Use a sharp pencil or a paper punch.
4. Hold the lid with the rim facing up. Push the eight pieces of yarn through the eight holes of the underside of the lid.
5. Tie the end of each piece of yarn in a large knot. Make the knot bigger than the hole so the yarn will not slip through.
6. Punch two more holes on opposite edges of the lid.
7. Push one end of a large piece of yarn from the top of the lid through one hole. It should come out on the underside of the chime.
8. Tie a large knot.
9. Push the other end of the yarn through the other hole and knot it.
10. Hang the chime on the branch of a tree or in your window.

Seashell Candy Dish

What type of candy do you like? Candy bars, rock candy, candy canes, lollipops, jelly beans —there are an endless variety of delicious sweet treats. How about making a special dish for the candy you can't quite get to now, but will definitely eat later?

The next time you go to a beach or go shopping, look for a large clam shell. With a little paint you can turn it into a beautiful candy dish. Be careful! When Mommy sees it she will want to have it for her own. Then you might find yourself making two candy dishes instead of one.

Things You Need

1 large clam shell
poster paints
white kitchen cleanser
watercolor brush
3 beads or 3 small seashells
liquid white glue
clear nail polish

Let's Begin

1. Add some of Mom's white kitchen cleanser to your poster paints so they will stick to the inside of the shell.
2. Paint the entire inside of the shell a light blue for the sky. Let dry.
3. Paint green water, Fig. a.
4. When dry, paint in the boat's hull or bottom and the center mast, Fig. b.
5. Paint in the sails and a triangle-shaped flag, Fig. c.
6. Paint in a fluffy cloud and a bright sun, Fig. d.
7. With liquid white glue, stick three beads or three small seashells to the bottom of the shell, spacing them the same distance from one another, Fig. e. Dry overnight. The beads make a stand so the candy dish will not wobble when placed on a table.
8. To protect the painted scene in the shell, brush clear nail polish—the kind that Mom uses on her nails—all over it.
9. Let the shell dry, and your candy dish is ready to use.

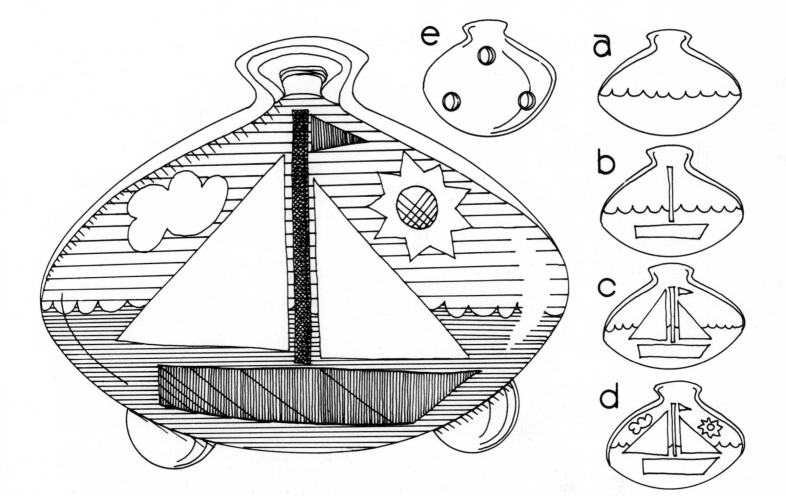

Braided Yarn Octopus

Imagine being an octopus and having eight arms! With all the chores you could get done at one time, you would be the most popular member of your family (with Mom and Dad at least). Well, what about an octopus for a friend? Not a real one, of course. It would have to live in a fish tank. The octopus you will make can go almost anywhere you go. *Except* in the water. Strange, isn't it?

Things You Need

1 package (skein) of colored yarn
1 sheet of cardboard
1 rubber ball
ribbon
scissors
liquid white glue
colored scraps of felt

Let's Begin

1. Wrap the entire package (skein) of colored yarn around a very long rectangular piece of cardboard, Fig. a. You can find cardboard of the right size behind the shirts Dad gets back from the laundry.
2. Clip a small piece of yarn off the free end of the wrapped yarn, and slip it under all the strands on one end of the cardboard.
3. Draw all the strands together on this end by tying a tight knot with the piece of yarn, Fig. a.
4. With the scissors, cut through all of the yarn at the other end of the cardboard, Fig. a.
5. Place the yarn, with the knotted part on top, over the rubber ball, Fig. b.
6. Push the yarn strands together so that the entire ball is covered.
7. Tie the yarn under the ball tightly with a piece of extra yarn, Fig. c.
8. Divide all the yarn under the head into eight equal parts.
9. Tie the eight sections very loosely to keep the yarn separated, Figs. c and d.
10. Take one section and divide it into three equal parts, Fig. e.
11. To braid the parts, study Figs. f and g. Number 1 strand-group goes over Number 2 (the strands on the left go over the middle strands). Then Number 3 strand-group goes over Number 1 (the strands on the right over the middle strands).
12. Repeat the operation, Number 2 strand-group going over Number 3 and so on, until you have just a little bit of yarn left on the bottom.
13. Tie the bottom of the braid with a piece of yarn or thin ribbon.
14. Braid the seven other arms of the octopus.
15. Tie a big bow under the octopus' head.
16. Glue on felt eyes and mouth with liquid white glue.

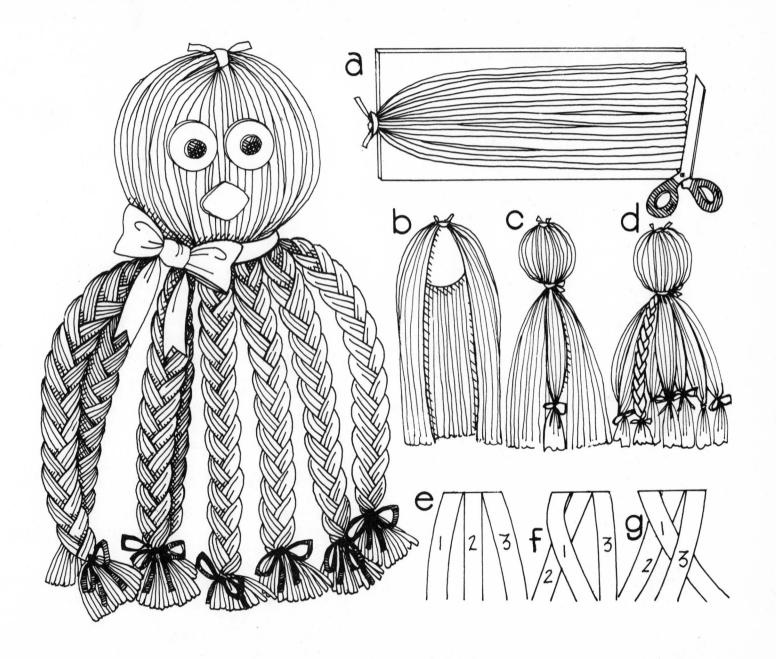

a

b c d

e 1 2 3 f 1 2 3 g 1 2 3

Sandcasted Footprint

Dinosaurs lived on the earth many years ago—some, maybe, in your back yard. When they were thirsty, they would go to a lake or stream for a drink. After they finished, they would go away, leaving their footprints in the mud. The mud turned very hard, and today, millions of years later, we can still see where the dinosaurs walked.

You can do the same thing the mighty dinosaur did long ago. For this project you will get your foot a little wet and sandy. No, you don't have to go down to the river for a drink before you start. It can be done in your bedroom and takes only a few minutes. Little enough time when you remember how many millions of years it took the dinosaur's footprints to make their own lasting impression.

Things You Need

shoe box
beach sand
coffee can
mixing spoon
aluminum foil
water
plaster of paris
your foot

Let's Begin

1. Press a sheet of aluminum foil into a shoe box, molding it to fit and cover the inside completely.
2. Fill the shoe box a little more than half full with sand.
3. Sprinkle the sand with water. Use a watering can or dip your fingers in a dish of water and sprinkle. Do not overwater. The sand should be just wet enough to hold together.
4. Place your bare foot in the sand and step down to form a footprint. Remove your foot.
5. Mix plaster of paris in an old coffee can.
6. Add water to the powder slowly while stirring. The plaster should have the consistency of a thin cream.
7. Pour the liquid plaster of paris into the footprint. Don't let it overflow the footprint impression.
8. Let the plaster dry for a week.
9. After a week, take out the hardened footprint. Brush away any loose sand.
10. Use it as a paper weight, for scaring people, or any way you want.

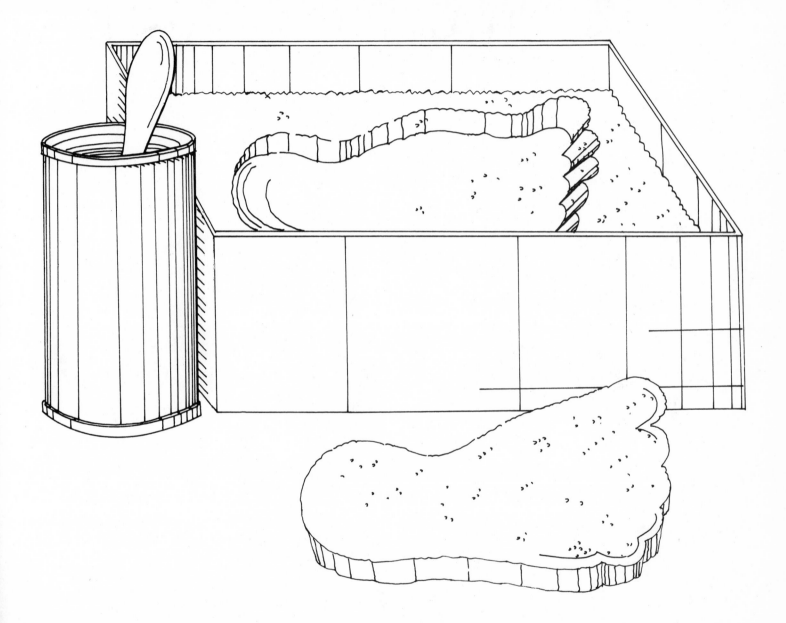

Huck Finn's Log Raft

Huckleberry Finn floated down the Mississippi. What sights he must have seen! Picture yourself on a river, passing farms, homes, and forests. When you are tired of being on the water, you set sail for the shore. The land is your home and the ground is your bed. You go to sleep by the comforting sound of a crackling fire . . .

Since you can't build a raft large enough for you to climb aboard, make a smaller one. Next time you are in the forest, or anywhere near trees, gather some twigs. With them, you can make a raft that will sail just as smoothly as Huck's did many years ago. Although your Mississippi may be a bathtub, you will still be captain of all you survey.

Things You Need

11 twigs of equal thickness
liquid white glue
1 sheet of white paper
colored crayons or colored felt-tipped markers
wax paper

Let's Begin

**1. Break or cut the twigs a little longer than the logs shown in the illustration.

2. Place six of the twigs on a sheet of wax paper. Glue the twigs together with the liquid white glue to form the raft, Fig. a.

**3. Break or cut two twigs to fit the width of the six glued twigs, Fig. b.

4. Glue these two twigs near the ends of the raft, Fig. b.

5. Let the raft dry overnight. When dry turn upside down.

**6. Cut a twig to form the mast and glue it, standing up, to the center of the raft.

**7. Cut the last two twigs to fit the width of the raft.

8. Glue the remaining two twigs to both sides of the mast, Fig. c.

9. Dry overnight.

10. Cut the sail from white paper. With crayon or marker, draw the letters H and F (*H*uckleberry *F*inn) on it, or use your own initials.

11. Push the paper sail through the standing twig, Fig. d. You are now ready to sail.

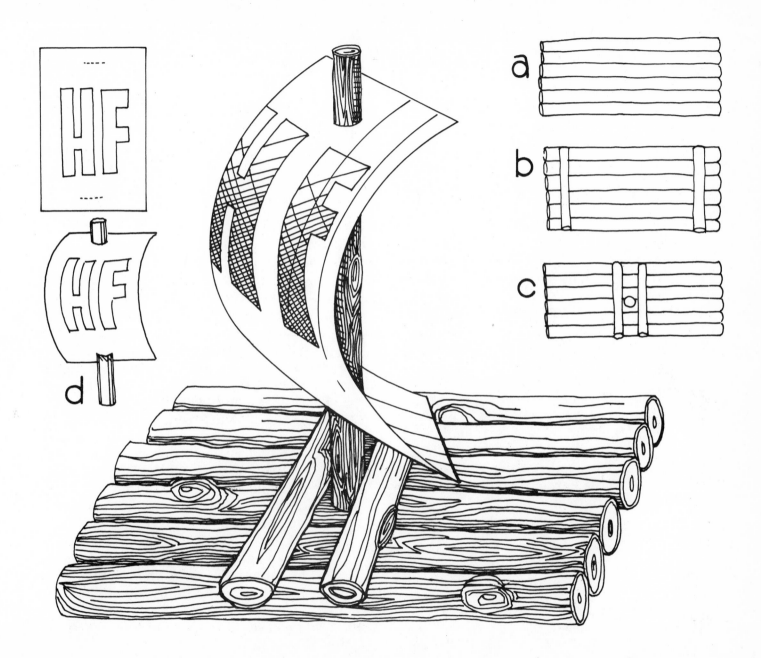

Slowpoke Stone Turtle

It was indeed the turtle who won the race. The hare thought he was the best, but the turtle kept a steady pace and came in first. Turtles don't move very quickly on the ground, but they can swim fast in the water. They carry their house on their backs. On land, it's a heavy load.

The Slowpoke Stone Turtle is as slow as the best of them. He won't move along the ground very well or in the water, but he will look very pretty on a table or in Mom's room. Before you start making the turtle, find his house. Look for a large, smooth stone in the woods, at the beach, or in the garden. When you find the best stone, you are ready to begin.

Things You Need

1 large, smooth stone
poster paints
watercolor brush
6 wood ice-cream spoons
liquid white glue

Let's Begin

1. Paint the large, smooth stone with green poster paint.
2. When dry, paint a light green shell design on the top of the stone.
3. Paint circles or shell markings on top of the shell design.
4. Turn the stone upside down when dry.
5. Paint the spoons green.
6. Make the turtle's head and tail by gluing the handle of one spoon onto the "bowl" of another, Fig. a. Glue both spoons to the stone as shown.
7. Make the front legs by gluing the handles of two spoons to the handle of the spoon that forms the head, Fig. b.
8. Make the back legs by gluing the handles of the last two spoons to the "bowl" of the spoon that forms the tail, Fig. c.
9. Dry overnight.
10. Add two eyes to the head of the turtle with white paint.

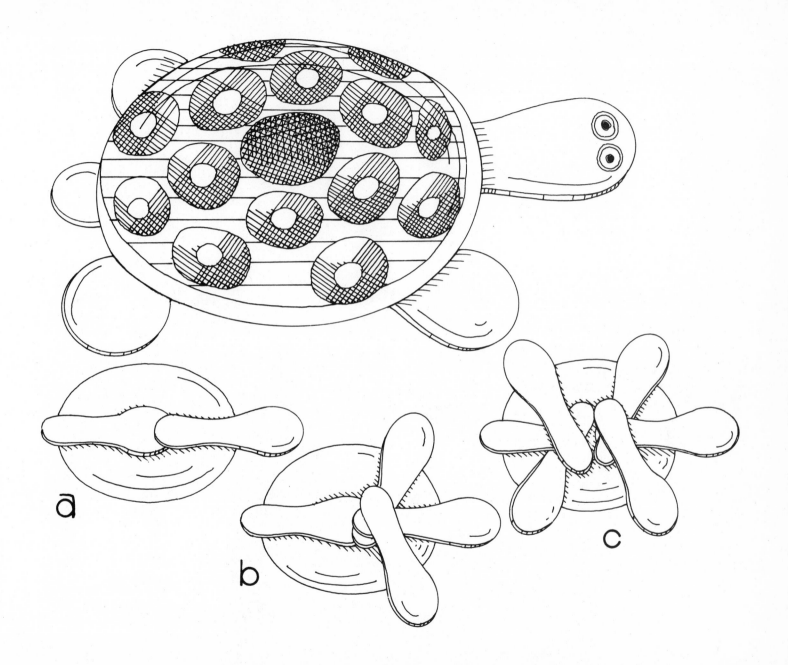

a

b

c

Crazy Stones

When you are at the beach, by a stream, or in the woods, look for small, smooth stones. Gather a whole bunch of them. With them, you can make many happy, funny, or nutty things. Give the Crazy Stones as gifts, trade them with your friends, or—why not keep them all for yourself?

Things You Need

small, smooth stones
poster paints
watercolor brush
colored construction paper
crayons or colored felt-tipped markers
liquid white glue

Let's Begin

The following are examples of Crazy Stones you can make. Follow them, or invent your own designs. In all cases, you will be drawing or painting on a stone.

- Draw a flower and glue a green paper leaf next to it, Fig. a.
- Draw a funny face and glue bits of yarn to the top for hair, Fig. b.
- Write your name, or the name of someone special, Fig. c.
- Draw symbols: stars, circles, lines, etc., Fig. d.
- Make a lovenote to Mom with a heart. Write "I Love You" in the heart, Fig. e.
- Draw a lion face. Glue a scalloped circle cut from orange paper to the back of the stone, Fig. f.
- Paint a clown face and glue a colored construction paper triangle on top of it for a hat, Fig. g.
- Draw a happy face, Fig. h.

a
b
c
d
c
f
g
h

Flowers, trees, and other growing things

Flowers, trees, and other growing things

In the words of a song written long before you were born, ". . . the best things in life are free." Just what does that mean?

Go outside and look around. If you're not a city kid, chances are you'll see some sky, a tree or two, the wavy grass. These are the things you couldn't buy for all the money in the world. People put prices on things as if that told you what they were worth. A tree makes you feel somehow more real. There's no money you can get that will buy that feeling.

You may not be able to enjoy nature whenever you want, but you can bring a bit of its beauty indoors. Or you can let it inspire you to imitate it in "made" things—almost as good. Some of the projects in this section call for actual materials from nature; some require things found in a store. All the projects should give you some sense of the great outdoor world—you'll even be able to sow your own grass seed and watch it grow.

Wax Leaf Collage

Look out of your window and you will see one of nature's most beautiful creations, the leaf. Leaves come in all sizes and shapes. How pretty they look on the trees! It's as if the trees are wearing fluttery green cloaks.

You can bring part of a tree into your bedroom. (No, you won't be hoisting the stump of a giant oak through the window.) You are going to make a beautiful leaf collage. This craft will make a lovely present for someone special, and looks really great when the light shines through it.

Things You Need

leaves of different shapes and sizes
2 sheets of waxed paper
crayons
butter knife or crayon sharpener
glitter
a clothes iron (ask Mom)

Let's Begin

1. Place the leaves on a sheet of waxed paper.
2. Remove the protective paper covering from the crayons.
3. Scrape crayon shavings over the leaves, or sharpen crayons, allowing shavings to fall on them.
4. Sprinkle glitter over the leaves and crayon shavings.
5. Cover this collage of leaves, glitter, and crayon shavings with a second sheet of waxed paper.
6. Ask Mom where you can iron your leaf collage.
**7. Iron over the waxed paper using a medium hot iron.
8. Let all the wax melt into the leaves. Your collage is now permanent. Hold it up to the window and see how beautiful it looks.

Eggshell Garden

Whoever thought that eggshells could be used as flower pots? You can't really grow flowers or trees in them, but you *can* grow grass. (Your Mom will be more than happy to supply you with the empty eggshells you need—she has been throwing them away for years.) It will be very exciting to see the grass grow higher and higher. When it's time to cut it, don't use a lawnmower. Scissors will do the trick.

Things You Need

1 broken eggshell

1 small piece of sponge
grass seed (available at garden supply stores)
water

Let's Begin

1. Place the piece of sponge into the eggshell, Fig. a. Wet the sponge.
2. Sprinkle grass seed on top of the sponge, Fig. b.
3. Sprinkle a little water on the sponge every day, Fig. c.
4. The grass should start growing in a week, Fig. d.

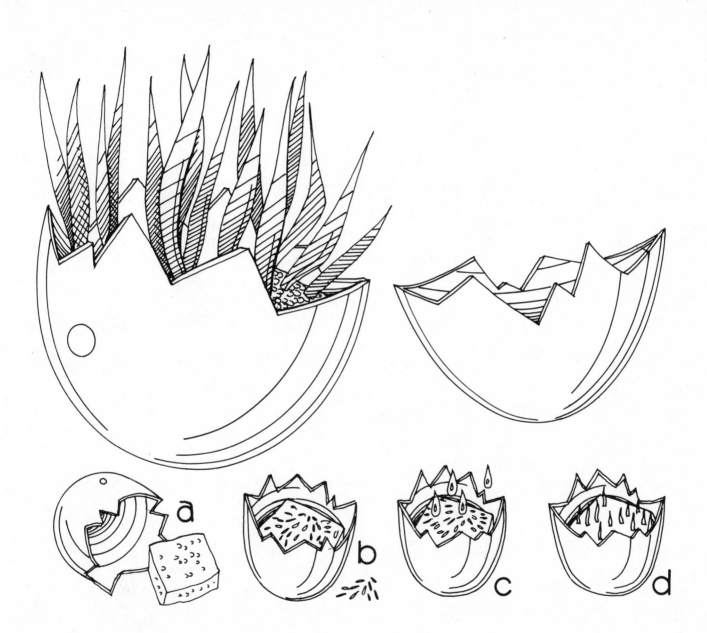

Oak-Leaf Seed Painting

For thousands of years people have been writing and drawing. Prehistoric man made paintings of animals on the walls of his cave. Some American Indians wrote on rocks. Today we write and draw on paper mostly. And what do we use to do it? Pens, pencils, crayons, chalk, and paintbrushes.

Now you are going to "draw" with seeds. The seeds you'll need are found in fruits like watermelon, cantaloupe, or honeydew melon. Save as many as you can, and let them dry thoroughly. (You can see that this craft has some good eating as well as good "making" involved in it.) You will also need some of Mom's spice seeds—things like poppy or fennel seeds. With this grain palette you are ready to take a giant step forward in the drawing history that caveman began.

Things You Need

dried watermelon, cantaloupe, and honeydew
  melon seeds
seeds from Mom's spice rack, like poppy,
  fennel, caraway or mustard seed
liquid white or brown glue
1 small cup
1 sheet of typewriter paper
paper paste
pencil
scissors
1 sheet of tracing paper
watercolor brush

Let's Begin

1. Trace the oak design from the book onto a sheet of typewriter paper.
2. Paste the paper with its tracing onto a sheet of cardboard with paper paste.
3. Pour liquid white or brown glue into a small paper cup.
4. Use a watercolor brush to brush glue into one area of the design, for example, an oak leaf.
5. Arrange the large seeds (watermelon or cantaloupe seeds) along the outline of the glued area first, then work them inward until the whole space is filled.
6. To work with the smaller seeds (poppy or fennel seeds), merely sprinkle seeds onto the glued area and blow away any that do not stick. Proceed to glue and fill all areas in the way that pleases you most.

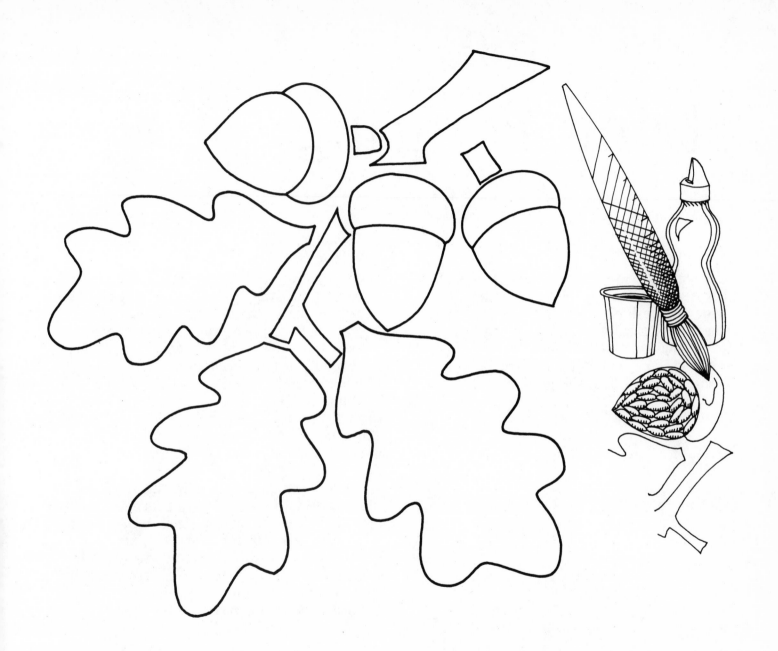

Vegetable String Painting

In Mexico they make paintings of string. They use different colored yarns, and make wonderful designs with it. You can do the same type of craftwork. It's a lot of fun seeing how string can be turned into very pretty vegetables. All you have to do is follow the directions. They will look good enough to eat.

Things You Need

1 sheet of tracing paper
pencil
scissors
paper paste
liquid white glue
paper cup
watercolor brush
scraps of colored knitting yarn
1 sheet of colored construction paper

Let's Begin

1. Trace the four vegetables from the book onto a sheet of tracing paper. The carrot is Shape a; the ear of corn, Shape b; the beet, Shape c; the pea pod, Shape d.
2. Cut the vegetables from the tracing paper and paste one or all of them onto a sheet of colored construction paper.
3. Pour some glue into a paper cup. Brush glue into the carrot, Shape a.
4. Put the string into the wet glue along the outline of the design.
5. Start outlining the carrot and work your way in.
6. Keep working the yarn in until you have filled the entire shape. Don't forget to work yarn in the carrot top "coil." Use a contrasting color of yarn for this part.
8. Proceed in a similar fashion with the other vegetables. Remember to differentiate by color the kernels of corn (the squares inside the corn) and the peas inside the pod.

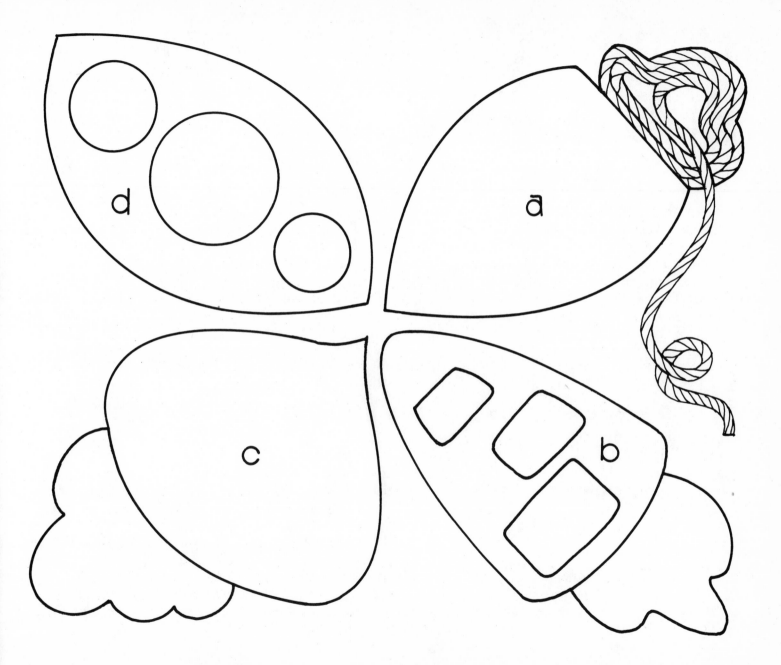

Papier-Mâché a Super Strawberry

What's your favorite fruit? If it's strawberries, then you're in luck. Even if you don't like this sweet fruit, you'll want to have one of these super berries. You won't find this one in your garden or even in a jar of strawberry jelly. If you did, it would probably take you two weeks just to eat it. This strawberry will be the center of attraction in your bedroom.

Things You Need

1 round balloon
string
newspaper
wallpaper or flour paste
poster paints
large watercolor brush
green construction paper
scissors

Let's Begin

1. Blow up a round balloon and tie the end.
2. Rip up newspaper into small strips.
3. Make a paste from the wallpaper paste or from cooking flour and water. In either case, add water slowly to the dry substance while you stir. You want the paste to be the consistency of soft mashed potatoes. Don't add too much water.
4. Dip the strips of newspaper into the paste.
5. Place a pasted strip on the balloon, Fig. a.
6. Keep pasting strips of newspaper over the balloon until it is covered.
7. Repeat the operation with a second layer of newspaper strips, Fig. b.
8. And with a third.
9. Remove the extra paste from the paper on the balloon with your fingers.
10. Let the balloon dry for one to two days.
11. When dry, paint the balloon with white poster paint. Let dry.
12. Paint the balloon again, this time with red poster paint. Let dry.
13. Paint in brown seeds.
14. Cut the strawberry leaf from green construction paper. Cut the paper in the shape of a circle.
15. Cut wedges out along the circle's perimeter, Fig. c.
16. Poke a hole in the center of the leaf.
17. Push the balloon's rubber "stem" through the hole. Your Super Strawberry is complete.

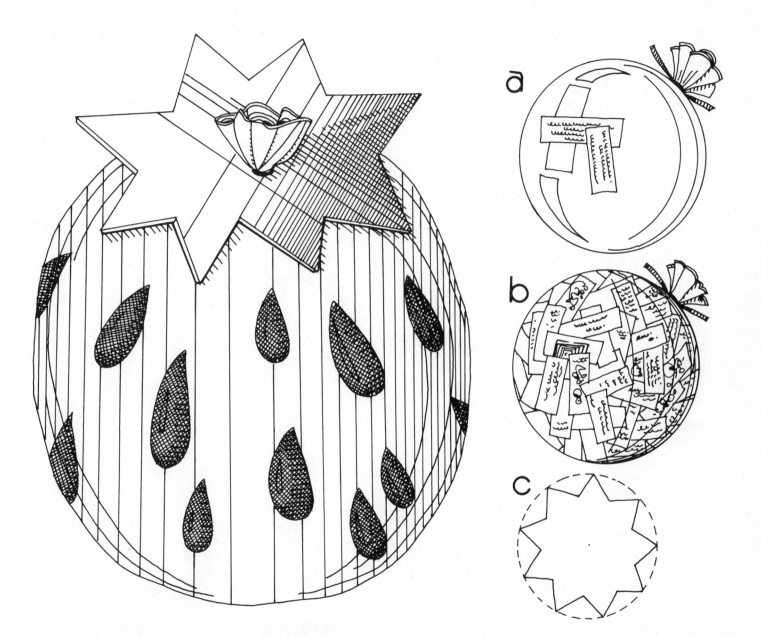

Embroider
a Special Flower

If you like to paint with string you will really like to learn how to embroider. Embroidering is a lot of fun once you've mastered a few basic stitches. You can't wait until your stitching is finished. This is a long project, so you might as well get started right now.

Things You Need

1 sheet of tracing paper
pencil
scissors
yellow, brown, and green embroidery thread
1 needle with a wide eye
1 piece of scrap fabric
embroidery hoop
safety pins

Let's Begin

Preliminaries

1. Ask Mom to help you find an embroidery hoop at the five-and-dime store.
2. Cut a piece of fabric larger than the hoop.
3. If the fabric is thin enough to see through, trace the flower from the book onto the fabric before you put it on the hoop. Fit it onto the hoop.
4. If you cannot see through the fabric, first trace the flower onto a sheet of tracing paper.
5. Put the fabric onto the hoop. Trim the tracing of the flower to the size of the fabric showing in the hoop.
6. Use safety pins to pin the tracing paper with design onto the fabric.
7. Embroider the design right through the tracing paper.
8. When all the design has been embroidered, pull away all of the tracing paper.
9. Remove your embroidery from the hoop.

Stitching the Fabric

Once the design is on the fabric, and the fabric on the hoop, you will start to embroider. Proceed with the following stitches:

The Outline Stitch

A. Fig. a shows the outline stitch in action. Use it to embroider the petals. To do the stitch, first thread the needle with yellow thread, and knot the end.**
B. Push the needle through the fabric from under the hoop. Make the needle come out on the outline of the petal.
C. Push the needle back through the fabric along the same line, making a small stitch.
D. Push the needle up through the fabric

(continued on page 76)

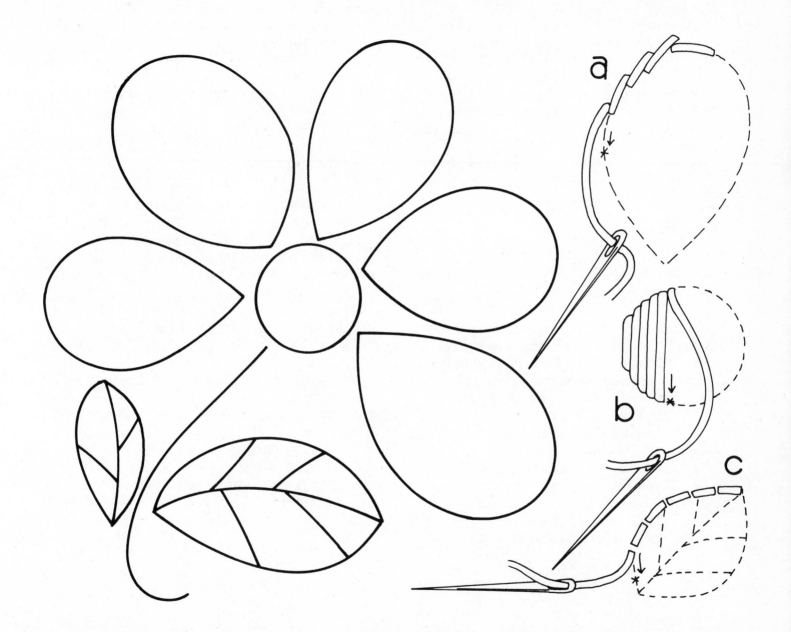

a

b

c

again. Make it come out to the left of the bottom of the stitch you just made.

E. Push the needle back through the hoop, following the line. You will have just made another stitch.

F. Do the rest of the stitches in the same way. Cover the entire outline of the petal with stitches.

G. After the last stitch, sew the thread under one stitch on the underside several times.

H. Cut the extra thread.

The Satin Stitch

A. Fig. b shows the satin stitch in action. Use it to make the bud. To do the stitch, first thread the needle with brown thread, and knot the end.**

B. Push the needle through the fabric from under the hoop. Make the needle come out on the bottom left of the circle's outline.

C. Push the needle back through the fabric on the line at the top of the circle, making a stitch across the circle.

D. Push the needle up through the fabric again. Make it come out on the top line of the circle to the immediate right of the stitch you just made.

E. Push the needle back through the fabric on the bottom line of the circle, making a stitch back across the circle. You have just

made two stitches. They should be close to each other.

F. In this manner, fill in the entire bud with stitches.

G. After the last stitch, sew the thread under one stitch on the underside several times.

H. Cut the extra thread.

The Running Stitch

A. Fig. c shows the running stitch in action. Use it to make the leaves and stem. To do the stitch, first thread the needle with green thread, and knot the end.**

B. Push the needle through the fabric from under the hoop. Make the needle come out on the outline of a leaf or the stem.

C. Push the needle back through the fabric on the same line, making a small stitch.

D. Push the needle up through the fabric again. Make it come out on the line, with a little space between it and the preceding stitch.

E. Push the needle back through the fabric on the line, making a small stitch as before.

F. Cover all outlines of the leaves and stem with this stitch.

G. After the last stitch, sew the thread under one stitch on the underside several times.

H. Cut the extra thread.

Link a Daisy Chain

You'll look as fresh as a daisy with a daisy chain around your neck. But that's not all you can do with this craft. If you make the chain long enough, it can border your mirror. You can even string chains all around your bedroom. Daisy chains are so bright and cheerful, no matter where you put them it will seem like a sunny spring day.

Things You Need

1 sheet of tracing paper
pencil
scissors
white, yellow, and green construction paper
paper paste

Let's Begin

1. Trace the flower, Shape a, from the book onto a sheet of tracing paper.
2. Cut out the tracing and, using it as a pattern, trace the flower onto white construction paper as many times as you will want flowers.
3. Trace the bud, Shape b, from the book onto tracing paper.
4. Cut out the tracing and, using it as a pattern, trace the bud onto yellow construction paper multiple times.
5. Trace the leaf, Shape c, onto tracing paper.
6. Cut out the tracing and, using it as a pattern, trace the leaf onto green construction paper multiple times.
7. Cut out all the flowers, buds, and leaves, from the construction paper.
8. Cut along the dotted lines on the flowers, (Fig. a) to form the petals.
9. Paste the buds to the center of the flowers.
10. Paste a flower to a flower at the ends.
11. Glue the flowers into a circle large enough to fit over your head or as large as you want to make the chain.
12. Glue the leaves onto the underside of some of the flowers.

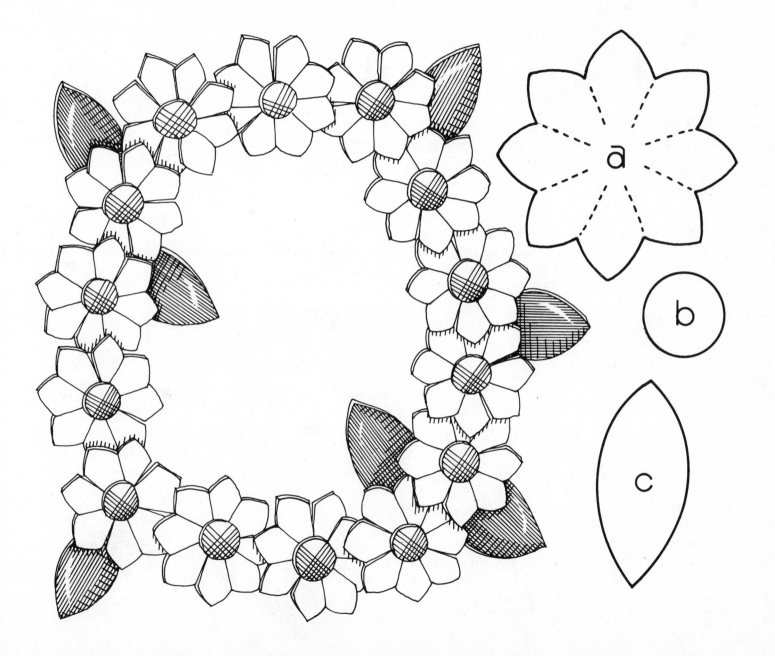

a

b

c

A Bouquet of Dried Flowers

Nothing can be as beautiful as a fresh flower "growing" in a vase. But fresh flowers are not always available. Why not try a bouquet of dried flowers?

Pick some of your favorite flowers when they are in bloom. (If they are in your garden, better ask Mom or Dad if it's okay.) Gather as many as you like. Then dry them following the directions below. The flowers will add a touch of beauty to wherever you put them.

Things You Need

summer or autumn flowers
string
scissors
1 wire coat hanger

Let's Begin

1. Remove most of the leaves of the flowers you have gathered, but leave the stems on.
2. Tie the flowers together at the stems with a string. Be sure the knot is tight.
3. Tie the string to a wire coat hanger.
4. Hang the flowers in a dark, dry place like a closet or an attic for about two weeks. Some flowers will dry better than others.
5. Untie the dry flowers and put in a vase.

Animals
are friendly
friends

Animals are friendly friends

"A man's best friend is his dog." You may wonder why this is true. It's simple. Dogs are very friendly animals. They love their owners and their owners love them. You have lived with your Mom and Dad for many years. During this time you have grown to love them. They give you food, comfort, and a place called home. It's a matter of love. A person who owns a dog gives him the same things. He takes care of the dog, and the dog gives him companionship in return.

Do you have a pet? Many people enjoy having an animal around the house. It's like having an extra brother or sister to play with. (Sometimes it's better.) Turtles, fish, birds, cats, even alligators and raccoons make wonderful pets. How nice it is to have an animal friend to fondle, love and talk to. Most animals like to hear the sound of your voice, even though they don't know what you are talking about. If you talk softly to them, they will be friendly to you.

What if you don't have a pet? If you like animals, you can have a roomful of friendly friends anyway. No, these aren't live creatures, but they look so good it's like having a zoo right in your bedroom. Just read the following sections and make a collection of animals all for yourself.

Silly Salt-Box Animals

If you walk into the woods you'll never see a raccoon, a deer, and a rabbit together. Animals like to live with their own kind. You can change this by making a collection of salt-box animals. With them, all kinds of animals will spend many happy hours sitting together on top of your dresser. You will enjoy playing games with them.

Things You Need

3 salt, oatmeal, or kitchen-cleanser containers
colored construction paper
pencil
scissors
tape
paper paste

Let's Begin

1. Cut a piece of white or colored construction paper as tall as your container.
2. Wrap this piece of paper around the container, Fig. a.
3. Tape the paper in place, Fig. b.
4. Outline the top of the container on the same colored paper with a pencil, Fig. c.
5. Cut out this circle.
6. Paste the circle on top of the container, Fig. d.
7. Cut out animal faces like the ones in the book.
8. The raccoon has black pointed ears, a brown nose, and a red mouth.
9. The monkey has a brown face, white eyes, a black nose, and a red mouth. To make the ears, cut a construction-paper circle in half.
10. The rabbit has long white ears with smaller pink ears inside them. Make a pink nose, red mouth, pink cheeks, and a purple bow tie from construction paper.
11. Put the faces on the containers with paper paste.

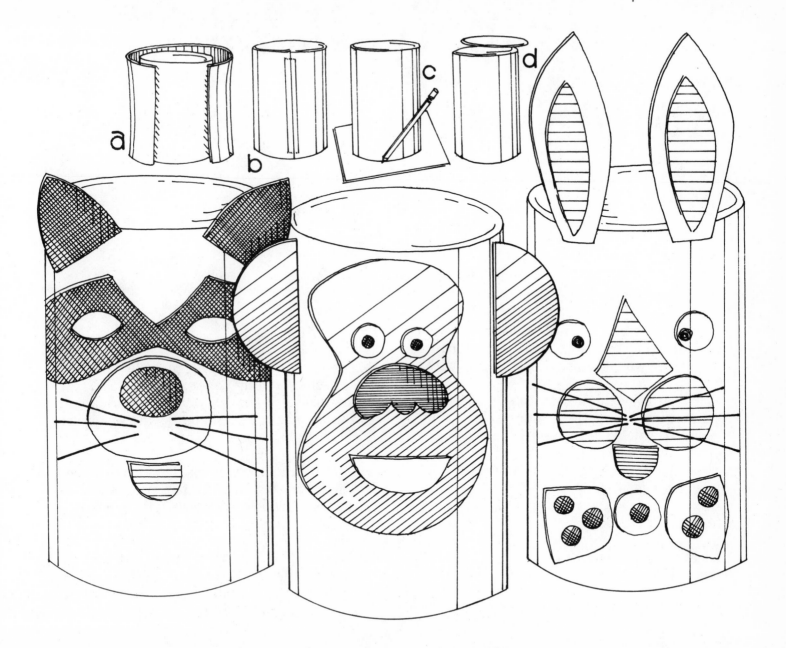

The Grapefruitiest Animal

Do you like grapefruit? It doesn't taste as sweet as other kinds of fruit. Grapefruit is good to eat when you are sick in bed with a cold.

Did you ever think that you could be best friends with one of these sour yellow fruits? Well, you can. All you need is a well-shaped grapefruit, some paper, and a few other things. It will be the most interesting pet you've ever seen.

Things You Need

1 sheet of tracing paper
pencil
scissors
colored construction paper
1 grapefruit
toothpicks

Let's Begin

1. Trace all of the shapes from the book onto a sheet of tracing paper: the eyes, Shape a; the noses, Shape b; the mouths, Shape c; half a mustache, Shape d; the eyebrows, Shape e; the cheeks, Shape f; and the ears, Shape g.
2. Cut out all shapes from the tracing paper.
3. Using the tracings as patterns, trace all shapes onto colored construction paper.
4. Cut out the colored face shapes with a scissors.
5. Pin a silly animal face onto the grapefruit with toothpicks. Mix up the face shapes. Keep your grapefruit animal in the refrigerator when you are not playing with it.

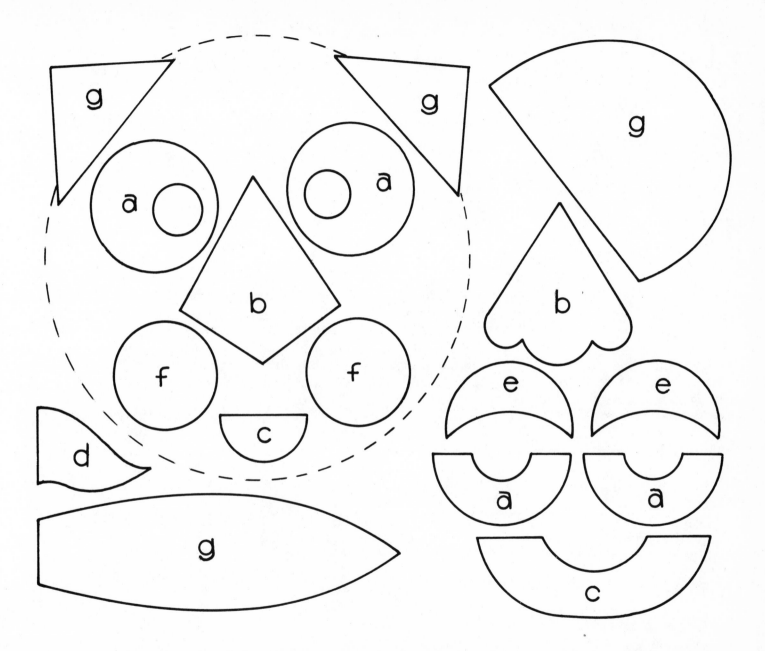

Rocking Horse

You don't see too many horses nowadays. People in the country see horses, and use them on their farms. If you don't have your own horse, now is the time to make one. With some paper and glue you can make a horse that rocks back and forth. Put it on the floor and imagine you are riding across the wide open fields.

Things You Need

1 sheet of tracing paper
pencil
scissors
colored construction paper
white glue or paper paste

Let's Begin

1. Trace the horse from the book onto a sheet of tracing paper.
2. Cut out the tracing and the shape inside the tracing which separates the horse from his rocker.
3. Using the tracing as a pattern, trace the horse shapes onto colored paper twice.
4. Cut out the construction-paper horses and cut along the lines on the neck.
5. The two shapes will be joined together with paper boxes. To make a box, first cut out a strip of paper about as long as the horse is from nose to tail. It should be as wide as the dotted box on the horse (see book).
6. Cut out two strips and fold them into five parts, Fig. a.
7. Fold each into a four-sided box.
8. Glue each box closed.
9. Face both horse shapes in the same direction. Glue the two boxes between both horses at the places indicated by the dotted boxes (see book and Fig. b).

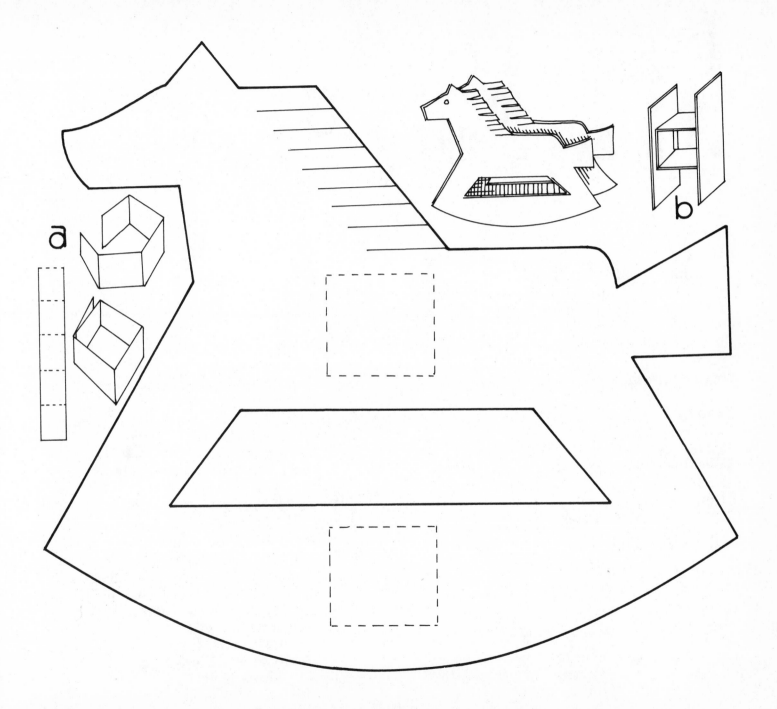

Plastic
Piggy Penny Saver

"Oink! Oink! Oink!" says the little pig. What he really means is: Save your pennies for a rainy day. The more pennies the piggy eats, the more fun you will have when he is full. When that happens—and the rain is falling—your pennies may be good for an exciting picture show.

Things You Need

1 gallon plastic bleach bottle
indelible felt-tipped markers
pink paper
1 pipe cleaner
1 sheet of tracing paper
pencil
scissors
4 thread spools made of wood
white liquid glue

Let's Begin

1. Wash the gallon plastic bleach bottle.
2. Place the bottle in front of you with the handle on top. Draw flower designs on it with the indelible felt-tipped markers.
3. Draw on an eye and a smiling mouth.
4. Trace the pig's ear, Shape a, from the book onto a sheet of tracing paper.
5. Cut out the tracing and, using it as a pattern, trace the ear shape *twice* onto pink paper.
6. Cut out the ears, and glue one to each side of the handle.
7. Punch a small hole in the middle of the bottom of the bottle using a sharp pencil.
8. Push a pipe cleaner into the hole. Use a dab of glue to hold the tail in place.
**9. Cut a slit on top of the bottle. Make sure it is big enough to let pennies drop in.
10. The legs of the piggy bank are made from the sewing spools. Glue the spools to the bottom or underside of the piggy bank with white liquid glue, Fig. b.
11. Let the glue dry overnight.
12. Unscrew the bottle cap—the pig's snout —when you want to borrow some pennies from the bank.

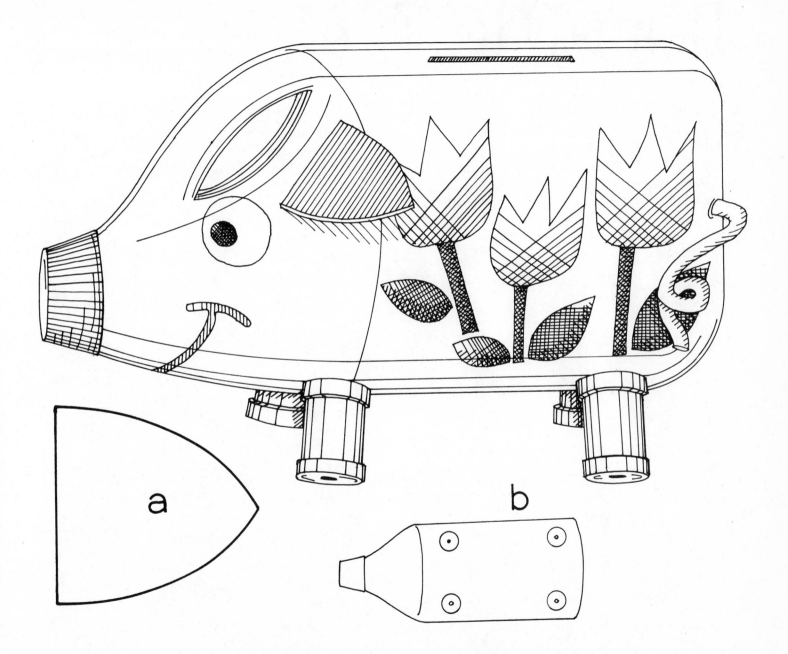

a

b

Bean-Bag Fun

Bean bags are fun to play with. The ones you are going to make are very special. They look like two of your favorite circus animals, the lion and the horse. Use these animal bean bags to play catch with your friends. They've probably never held a lion or a horse in their hands.

Things You Need

colored felt
drawing paper
pencil
needle
scissors
thread
dried beans

Let's Begin

Cut three felt squares for the horse Bean Bag; two for the Lion Bean Bag. All squares should be the same size.

The Horse Bean Bag

1. To make a horse-head pattern, first cut a piece of drawing paper to the same size as the felt squares.
2. Draw a diagonal line (a line from corner to corner) on the paper, Line P, Fig. a.
3. Draw a line across the width of the pa-per right in the middle, Line Z, Fig. a.
4. Draw another line across the width of the paper, this time halfway between Line Z and the top of the paper: Line O, Fig. a.
5. Draw a line from the top to the bottom of the paper, right in the middle: Line Y, Fig. a.
6. Fig. b shows how to draw the horse-head shape:
   draw a line from O to Y;
   draw a line from Z to X;
   draw a line from X to P.
   These lines are shown by the heavy lines in Fig. b.
**7. Pin the horse drawing onto one square of the felt.
8. Cut through the paper and the felt following the outline of the horse-head drawing, Fig. c.
9. Make the ear from a triangle of felt, and the mane from small felt rectangles. Use scrap felt for ears and mane.
10. To assemble the bean bag, first lay another of the felt squares on the table.
11. Put the ear on top of the felt square a little over the top edge, Fig. d.
12. Place the rectangles on top of the felt square, a little over the edge of the right-hand side, as shown, Fig. d.

(continued on page 94)

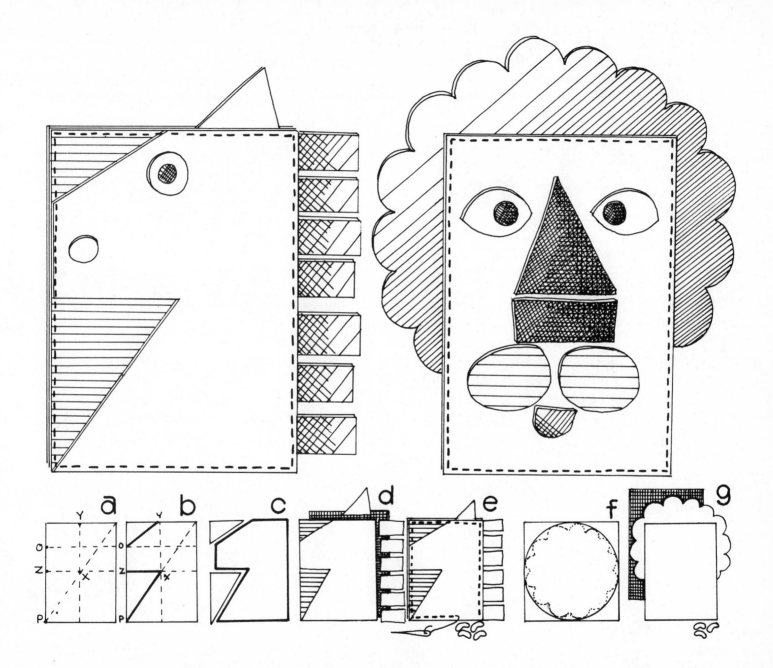

a b c d e f g

13. Lay the last square of felt on top of the other square, sandwiching the ear and mane between them.
14. Place the felt horse head shape on top of the bean bag, Fig. d.
**15. Pin everything in place.
**16. Thread a needle, and sew around the sides of the bag (see dotted line, Fig. e).
17. Leave a little part of the bag unsewn on the bottom, Fig. e.
18. Fill the bag halfway full with dried beans.
19. Sew the unsewn part of the bag closed. Go over the last stitch many times, then cut the thread.
20. Glue on round felt eyes and nose made from felt scrap.

The Lion Bean Bag

1. Cut a circle out of drawing paper which is larger than the size of the felt squares.

2. Scallop or cut out small circles along the edge of the large circle, Fig. f.
**3. Pin the scalloped circle onto felt and, following the outline, cut out felt replica. This will be the lion's mane.
4. Place the first felt square for the bean bag on the table.
5. Put the scalloped felt circle on top of the felt square. It should stick out above the top, Fig. g.
6. Place the second felt square on top of the scalloped circle, aligning it to the first square.
7. Sew the bean bag in the same manner as the horse, Fig. g, leaving open a little part of the bag, filling bag with beans, etc.
8. Cut lion's face shapes (see book) from felt and glue to top felt square of the bean bag. Use liquid white glue.

Join a Dancing Bear

One of the best loved acts in the circus is the dancing bears. These lumbering animals move about the ring with surprising grace. It looks as if their arms are hardly attached to them and are going to fall off any minute.

Now is your chance to have your own dancing bear. It comes apart and snaps together in seconds. You can carry your dancing friend in your pocket and amaze people with him wherever you go.

Things You Need

1 sheet of tracing paper
pencil
scissors
brown construction paper
5 large clothing snaps
colored scrap paper

Let's Begin

1. Trace onto tracing paper the bear's head, Shape a; the leg, Shape b; and the arm, Shape c.
2. Cut out the tracings from the paper. Using them as patterns, trace one head, two legs, and two arms onto brown construction paper.
3. Cut out all of the bear parts from the brown construction paper.
4. Make the body of the bear from a circle cut out of the same brown paper. Trace around a small dish to get the circle.
5. Cut out the circle.
6. Ask Mom for five large snaps.
7. Punch one side of the snap through the circle on the bottom of the head (see book).
8. Punch a tiny hole through the body near the edge of the circle.
9. Push the other half of the snap into this hole and, turning circle over, snap the head onto the body.
10. Punch two more holes through the body, one on either side of the head (see book). Punch holes in arms and snap to body.
11. Attach legs on the bottom of the circle, the same way as you did the arms.
12. Paste a paper nose, eyes, and mouth on the bear's face.

Circus Animal Car

The news is out: The circus is coming to town.

It's a very exciting time. The ringmaster, clowns, elephants, and cages of wild animals parade down Main Street. They are marching to the big top where you can see the Greatest Show on Earth.

It's a good thing the lions and tigers are in sturdy cages. You wouldn't want them to escape and scare everyone. You'd better make some animal cages for yourself. Why? Because later on you will make some wild animals, and they are going to need to be put behind bars!

Things You Need

small soap-powder boxes
cardboard
pencil
scissors
tracing paper
poster paints
paintbrush
brass paper fasteners
cellophane tape
colored construction paper

Let's Begin

**1. With scissors, cut open the top of a soap-powder box, leaving one short side uncut, Fig. a.

**2. Cut rectangles out of the box on one side, Fig. a. You can cut out as many rectangles as you want. Try to keep all the cutout shapes the same size and in a straight line.

3. Paint and decorate the box with poster paints. If the paint doesn't stick to the box, add some kitchen cleanser to the paint.

4. Make the four wheels from circles cut out of cardboard. Use a glass to trace the circles.

5. Paint the wheels a bright color.

6. Punch a hole through the center of each wheel with a sharp pencil point.

7. Punch four holes in your box where the wheels will be fastened. Locate the holes near the bottom and away from the ends of the box, Fig. a.

8. Push a paper fastener through the holes in the wheels and through the holes in the box. Fasten all four wheels to the box by spreading out the two prongs of the fastener.

9. Trace the handle shape from the book onto tracing paper.

10. Cut out the tracing and, using it as a pattern, trace the handle onto construction paper.

11. Cut out the handle and glue it to the side of the box.

12. Tape the flap closed when an animal comes to stay, Fig. b.

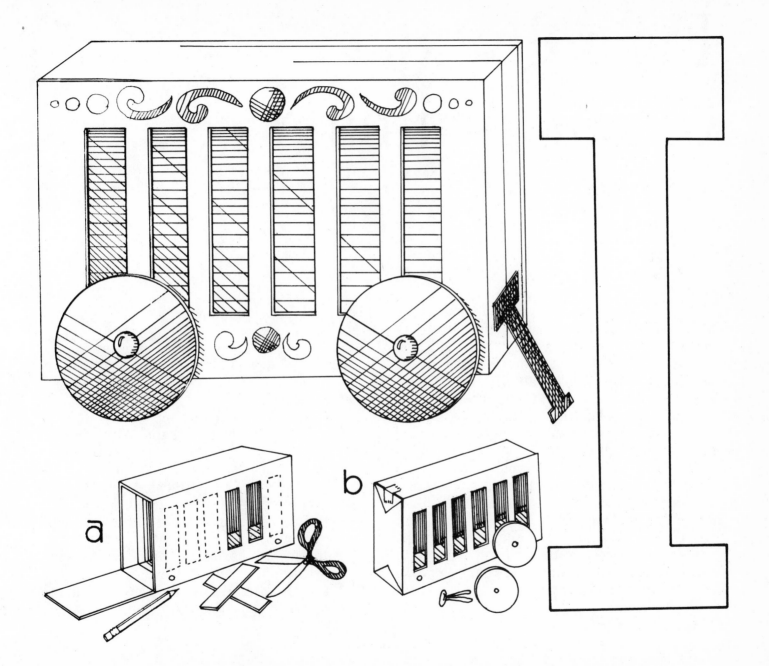

a

b

Friendly Circus Animals

These animals came all the way from Africa to be with you. That's where they live. The elephant and the giraffe like to eat the leaves in the trees. As you may imagine, the giraffe has it all over the elephant in treetop leaf-eating. The hippo couldn't care less about the two, preferring instead to staying in the cool river water. In the evening he goes for a nice grassy dinner on the shore.

Your three African animals should each have his own cage to live in (see preceding project). You might have to cut a hole in the top of one of the cages so that the giraffe can stretch his neck. The elephant and the hippo will fit very nicely in their new homes. With this new collection of animals, your room will be a circus of fun for you.

Things You Need

tracing paper

colored construction paper
cardboard
crayons or colored felt-tipped markers
tape

Let's Begin

1. Trace each animal shape onto tracing paper.
2. Cut out each tracing.
3. Using tracings as patterns, trace the animals onto colored construction paper.
4. Cut out the animals from the colored construction paper.
5. Add fun designs to each animal with colored felt-tipped markers or crayons.
6. Place an animal in each circus wagon.
7. Use a little tape to keep the animals standing.

Sugar and
spice
and everything
nice

Sugar and spice
and everything nice

What kind of little girl are you? Are you made of sugar and spice—of pinks and pastels, frills, bows, and jump ropes? Or of sterner stuff, like softballs and cowboys and tree-climbing? It's not ungirl-like to do big, active things—where would Alice have been if she hadn't told the Queen of Hearts' courtiers that they were nothing but a pack of cards?

Of course, the important thing is to be yourself and to enjoy as much as you can of every day. The projects in this section should help you to do just that. Whatever kind of girl you are, you probably like dolls, and this chapter should add a few beauties to your collection. Included here also are several items you can actually use, like the Little Moppet Hand Mirror, plus a découpage project that's really fun. Of course, if you see nothing in this section which especially interests you, why not skip to the next one for boys? There's no law around which says you can't build a robot or make a spooky totem pole . . .

Little Moppet Hand Mirror

You can turn your hand mirror into a very pretty little girl. Her name is Little Moppet. She's a young girl who likes being with you when you want to look pretty. When she is not with you, she deserves a place among your favorite play friends. From now on, there will be two pretty little girls in your room: you and Little Moppet.

Things You Need

plastic hand mirror
pink paper
crayons or colored felt-tipped markers
paper paste
scrap knitting yarn
1 piece of cardboard
scissors
liquid white glue
ribbon

Let's Begin

1. Make Little Moppet's hair by wrapping yarn around a small square of cardboard, Fig. a. About twelve "wraps" should do it.
2. Slip a short piece of yarn under the wrapped yarn on the cardboard and push to the end of the square.
3. Using the piece of yarn, tie all the yarn together in a tight knot.
4. Cut open the yarn coil at the bottom of the cardboard, Fig. b.
5. Make two more hair pieces as you did the above.
6. Cut a circle out of pink paper to fit the back part of the mirror, Fig. c.
7. Draw a face on the circle with crayons or colored felt-tipped markers.
8. Paste the circle to the back of the mirror, Fig. c.
9. Glue a hair piece to each side of the mirror, Fig. d.
10. Glue the last piece of hair to the top of the mirror, Fig. e.
11. Dry overnight.
12. Tie a bow with the ribbon onto the handle.

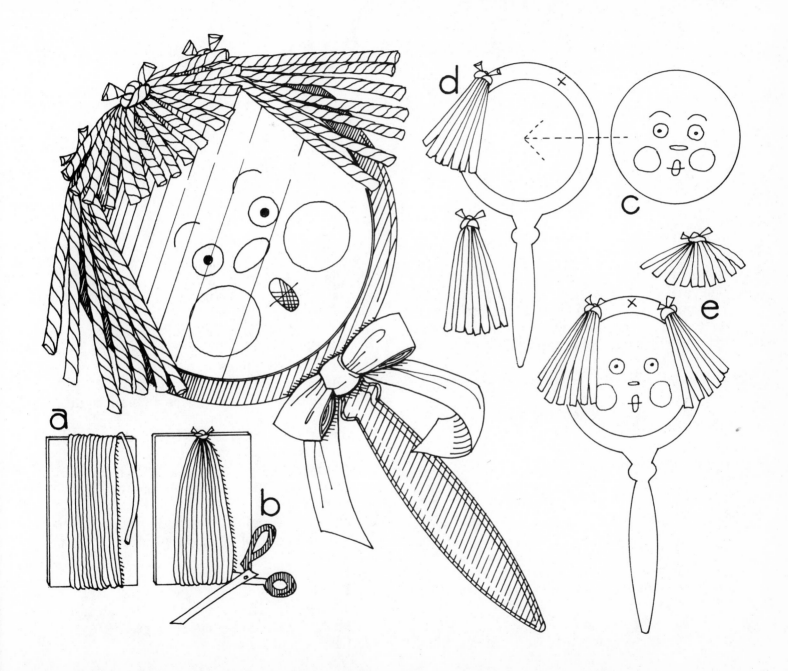

a

b

c

d

e

Tie a Yarn Doll

A marionette is a doll that has strings attached to it. A Yarn Doll has no strings but, as you might imagine, a lot of woolly yarn. The yarn forms the arms, legs, body, and head. You make the doll move without strings. In fact, she is at her best when given the chance to let her arms and legs dangle freely.

Things You Need

one 4-oz. package (skein) of yarn
small rubber ball
scissors
1 piece of cardboard
two small buttons

Let's Begin

1. Wrap the entire package of yarn around a long rectangle of cardboard.
2. Slip a short piece of yarn under the wrapped yarn on the cardboard and push to the end of the rectangle.
3. Using the piece of yarn, tie all the yarn together in a tight knot. Cut the yarn open at the bottom of the cardboard.
4. Place the knotted yarn over a small rubber ball. Keep the knot on top of the ball, Fig. a.
5. Arrange the yarn around the ball.
6. Tie the yarn under the ball in a tight knot with another piece of yarn, Fig. b.
7. Divide the hanging yarn in half.
8. Divide one of the halves in half again, Fig. c.
9. Tie these sections halfway down with small pieces of yarn.
10. Trim off the yarn from a little below the knots, Fig. d. You have just made the arms.
11. Tie the remaining yarn halfway down with another piece of yarn. Make a tight knot.
12. Divide the hanging yarn into two parts, Fig. e.
13. Tie each section near the bottom in a tight knot, Fig. f. These are the legs.
14. Glue on button eyes.

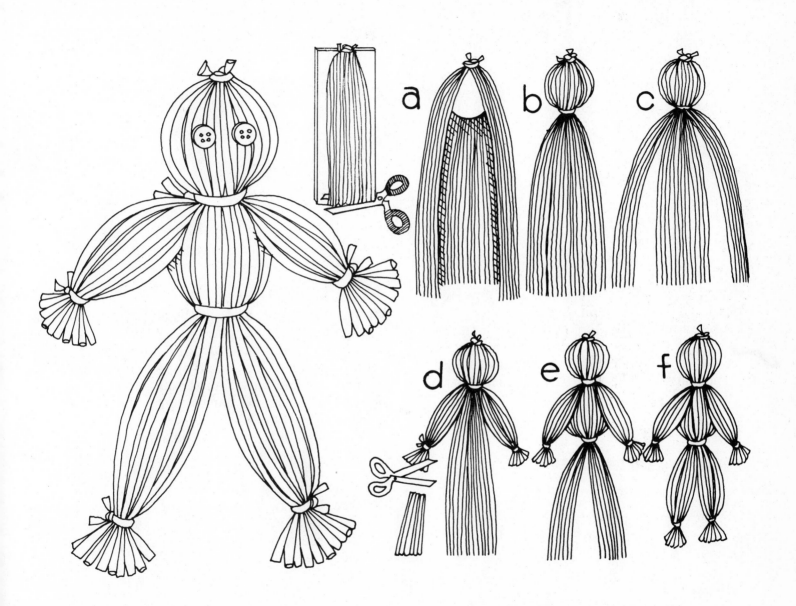

a

b

c

d

e

f

Hoop-Skirt Dottie

You may never own a hoop skirt, but why not make a doll that wears one? Your Hoop-Skirt Dottie doll stands very tall on her pretty round skirt. With her arms folded and her skirt in place, she will add a charming touch to your room. Be careful! A handsome young prince might take her away when you are asleep.

Things You Need

1 sheet of tracing paper
pencil
scissors
white drawing paper
crayons or colored felt-tipped markers
cellophane tape

Let's Begin

1. Trace the doll from the book onto a sheet of tracing paper.
2. Cut out the tracing.
3. Use the cutout to trace the doll shape onto white drawing paper.
4. Draw on hair, face, and dress designs with crayons or colored felt-tipped markers.
5. Cut the doll out from the paper.
6. Cut slits on the hands along the dotted lines (see book).
7. Cut slits on the tabs of the skirt along the dotted lines (see book).
8. Curl the skirt back. Fit one tab into the other tab, Fig. a.
9. Put a piece of tape on the tabs to hold them in place.
10. Curl the arms forward. Fit one slit into the other slit, Fig. b.

Découpage
a Jewelry Box

Do you know what découpage is? It is a way of decorating an object with pictures, photographs, and designs. (The designs are protected from dust and dirt under many layers of varnish.) You can découpage almost any smooth surface, like a wastepaper basket or a piece of wood. You can make many wonderful gifts for the people you love the most.

Your first découpage project will be something special for your room. You are going to make a very pretty jewelry box. Put your jewelry and any personal things you might have in this precious box, or give it as a special present to someone who'd like it.

Things You Need

1 cigar or gift box
poster paints
paintbrush
large paper doilies
scissors
liquid white glue
paper cup

Let's Begin

1. Paint the box any color you want with poster paints, Fig. a.
2. Let the box dry.
3. Cut a large doily into large and small designs, Fig. b.
4. Brush liquid white glue over the entire cover of the box, Fig. c. If your bottle of glue is too small to allow a paint brush to fit in, pour the glue into a paper cup.
5. Place the cut doilies on the glued surface. Use as many doily shapes as you wish, Fig. d.
6. Glue doily shapes to the sides.
7. Let the glue dry.
8. When dry, paint the entire box with liquid white glue.
9. Let the glue dry.
10. Brush at least four layers of glue on the box.
11. Let each layer of glue dry before you brush on the next layer. On your next project, instead of doilies try using magazine cutouts, small drawings, or scraps of torn paper.

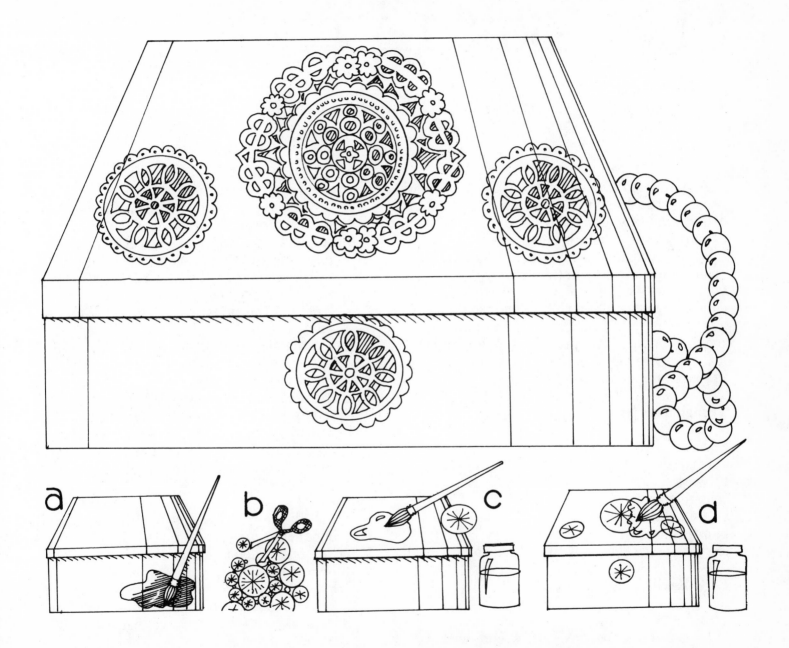

a

b

c

d

Shoe-Box Kitchen

Are you too young to cook? You probably are, but that doesn't mean you can't help Mom around the kitchen. There are many jobs you can do that will help her prepare a meal. It's a lot of fun using a stove and going to the refrigerator, but these are not toys you can play with. So why not make your own kitchen? You can have your very own stove and refrigerator and invite your friends over for a lesson in cooking. When you are old enough to have learned more about cooking, Mom will let you prepare supper for the family.

Things You Need

2 shoe boxes
cardboard
scissors
colored paper
white poster paint
paintbrush
crayons or colored felt-tipped markers

Let's Begin

THE REFRIGERATOR
1. Stand a shoe box on its end with the opening facing you.
2. Cut shelves from the cardboard the same size as the inside of the box.
3. Add a tab to both sides of each shelf before you cut out the shelves, Fig. a.
**4. Cut a slit into both sides of the box for each shelf (see book).
5. Push out the sides of the box to fit in the shelf, Fig. a.
6. Fit the tabs of the shelves into the slits in the sides of the box.
7. Paint the box white.
8. Add door handles with crayons or colored felt-tipped markers to the front cover.
9. Cut pictures of food from magazines or make different shapes using colored paper and store in your refrigerator.

THE STOVE
1. Lay the second box down with the opening facing up.
**2. Cut out a door on the side facing you. Follow the dotted line, Fig. b.
3. Paint the box white.
4. Cover the box and add knobs and top burners with crayons or colored felt-tipped markers.

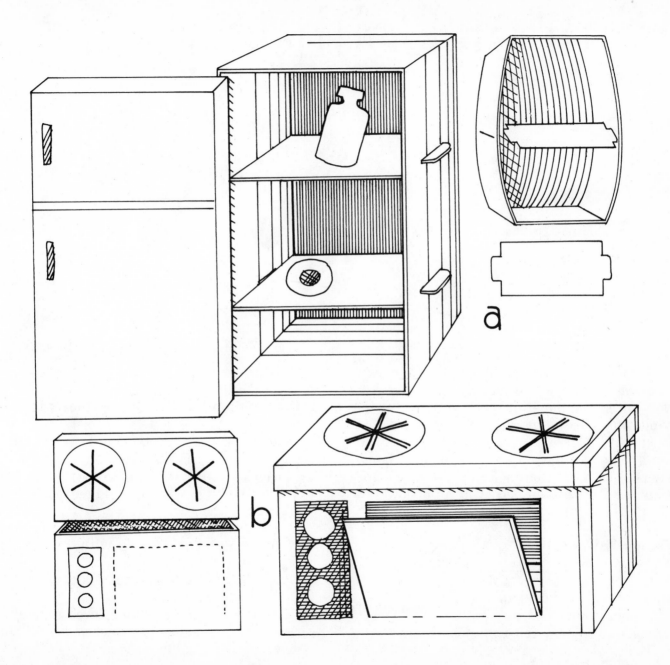

a

b

Build a Dollhouse

If you don't have a dollhouse of your own, make one. It's not as difficult as it looks. You won't need a hammer or nails, or glass for the windows. With four shoe boxes and a few sheets of colored construction paper, your small dolls can have a lovely two-story home. There'll be a kitchen, a living room, a bathroom, and a bedroom. All you need now is a family that wants to move in.

Things You Need

4 shoe boxes
colored construction paper
white liquid glue
crayons or colored felt-tipped markers

Let's Begin

1. Glue the four shoe boxes together with the open sides facing you (see book).
2. Fold in half two sheets of red construction paper as wide as the box front.
3. Place the folded sheets of construction paper on the table with the fold on top. These will make the roof.
4. Draw shingles and windows on both sides of the folded paper roofs with crayons or markers.
5. Glue (or tape) one sheet of folded paper to each of the top boxes.
6. Cut out tree shapes from colored construction paper, and glue one to each side of the house.

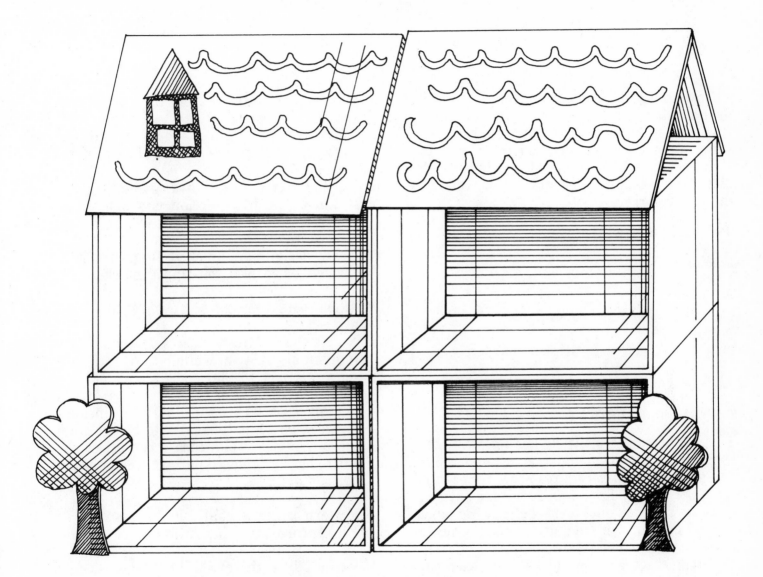

Folded Furniture

Now that you've got a dollhouse, it's time to make the furniture for it. Each piece of furniture is simple to make. All it takes is one strip of paper for each. You must fold the strips as shown in the drawings. Study the pictures. It is very important that you fold the paper correctly.

Things You Need

tracing paper
scissors
pencil
colored construction paper
paper paste
crayons or colored felt-tipped markers

Let's Begin

GENERAL INSTRUCTIONS

1. Each piece of furniture has its own letter pattern, its own illustration and corresponding figure. Figures show how to fold paper strips. Trace the furniture patterns from the book onto a sheet of tracing paper and cut out the tracings. (See specific instructions which follow.)
2. Using tracings as patterns, trace each pattern onto a different colored sheet of construction paper.
3. Cut out the patterns from the colored construction paper.
4. Following the figures (heavily outlined drawings), fold the strips. Paste strips closed along tabs.
5. Each strip requires four folds making five sections. The fifth section is shorter than the rest. This is the tab that will be pasted to close the strip.
6. Draw designs on finished furniture with crayons or colored felt-tipped markers.

WORKING THE PATTERNS

1. Notice that Patterns a, g, f-1, and f-2 are individually drawn, while b, c, d, and e are shown as part of a larger pattern block. To trace b, c, d, and e, use arrows as guides to a given pattern's width. Dotted lines indicate where a pattern should be cut from the larger block (Pattern e comprises the entire block). Fold all patterns along heavy horizontal lines.

   Pattern a is the chair. Fold as shown in Fig. a, furniture illustrations.

2. Pattern b is the clock. Fold as shown in Fig. b, furniture illustrations.
3. Pattern c is the television. Fold as shown in

118

(continued on page 121)

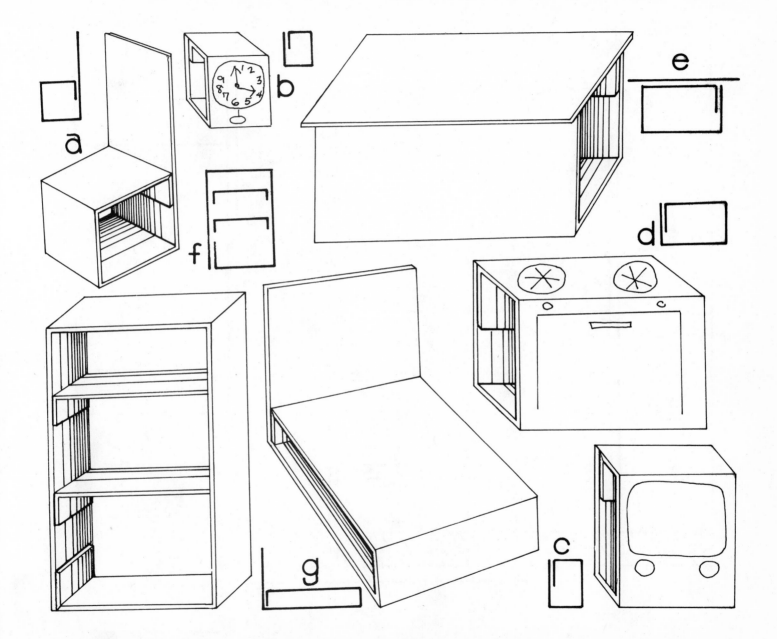

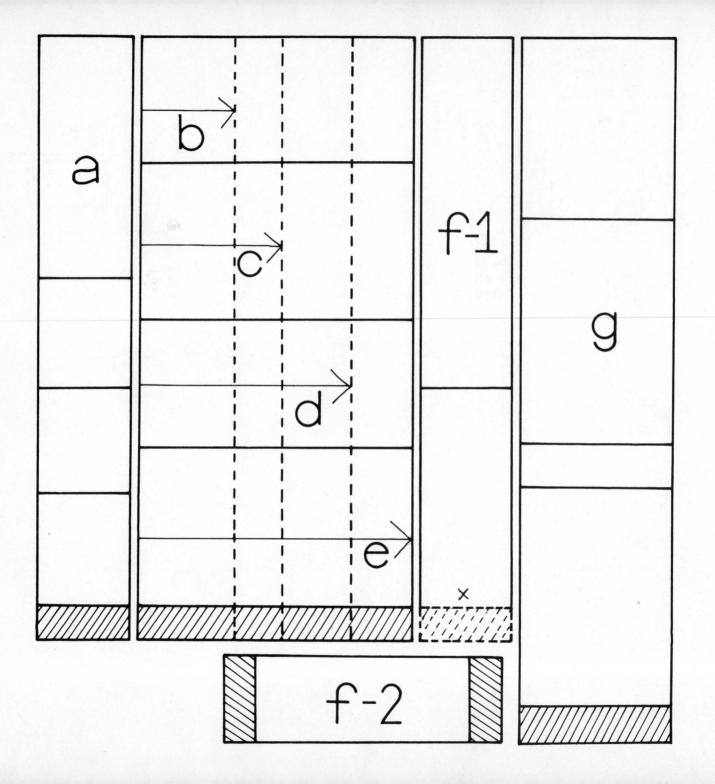

Fig. c, furniture illustrations.

4. Pattern d is the stove. Fold as shown in Fig. d, furniture illustrations.
5. Pattern e is the table base. Fold as shown in Fig. e, furniture illustrations. Make the table top from a small square of construction paper. Paste top to base.
6. Pattern f-1 is one-half the entire cabinet. Trace the pattern twice, end-to-end. That is, the larger rectangular segment of the first tracing should butt the shorter of the second (paste over tab at Point x). Fold as shown in Fig. f, furniture illustrations (one tab remains for closing the whole strip).
7. Pattern f-2 is the shelf. Make two shelves, and fit within cabinet, paste along bent tabs.
8. Pattern g is the bed. Fold as shown in Fig. g, furniture illustrations.

Snips, snails, and puppy dog tails

Snips, snails, and puppy dog tails

What is a little boy? A volcano of energy, a zoo keeper of wild animals, a Hall of Fame baseball player. Or maybe a movie director, a musician, the greatest chef in the world. What happened to the snips, snails, and puppy-dog tails? Any boy with a puppy-dog tail would probably find himself in a circus sideshow.

Boys are anything they want to be. They can catch fish or make furniture for the house. They like action—but they like to see and make beautiful things too. How do you feel, as a boy, when you hold a little kitten? Just as much yourself as when you swing that bat at a speeding fast ball or throw that fantastic pass. It's good to win, but it's also good to sit down and relax and start to work with your hands.

This chapter should provide an ample opportunity to do just that. There's a bug cage to make, a telescope, and even a milk-container village. You will have many hours of fun creating toys from objects that are usually thrown away. More to the point, you will have fun creating. Isn't that part of what being a boy is about?

Paper-Cup Army

You have to prepare your soldiers for a very important battle. You are the captain, and not one man must be lost. During the fighting you will be moving your soldiers around the battlefield so that you will win your make-believe war. When the big battle is over, you can put your soldiers away for another day of fun.

Your paper-cup army can be as large as you want it to be. Two different armies can be made by changing the color of the paper that is wrapped around the cups. Have a blue army fight a green army. If you win enough battles, you just might be a general before you know it.

Things You Need

8-oz. drinking cups (as many as you want)
colored construction paper
paper paste
tape
scissors

crayons or colored felt-tipped markers

Let's Begin

1. Wrap a piece of blue construction paper around a paper cup, Fig. a.
2. Tape the paper together around the cup.
3. With the scissors, trim all the extra paper that may go above and below the cup.
4. Make the face from a strip of pink, brown, or yellow paper. Cut it the size of the face in the book. Make it long enough to go around the top of the cup.
5. Wrap the face around the cup close to the top, Fig. b.
6. With crayons or colored felt-tipped markers, draw a face and a black hat brim on the strip (see book).
7. Paste a yellow paper feather onto the top of the cup.
8. Glue a red paper X to the front of the cup.
9. Cut out a triangle from the bottom of the cup to form the legs, Fig. c.

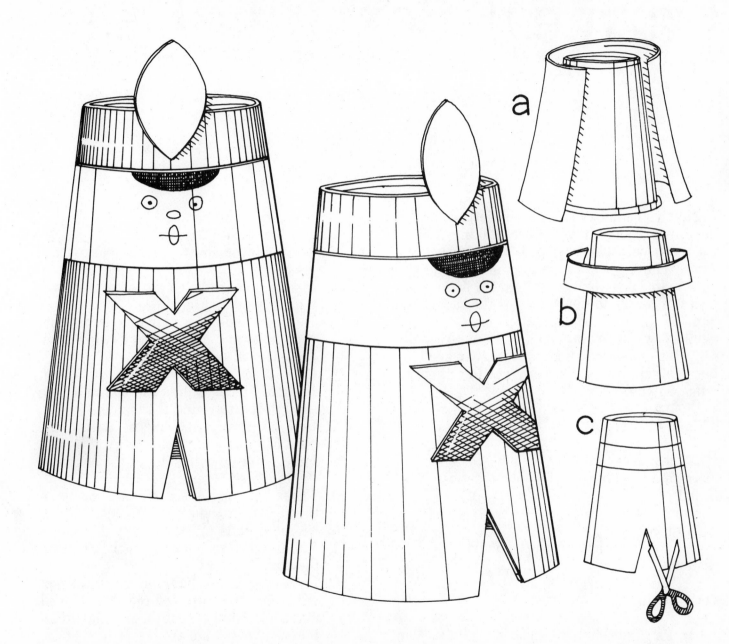

a

b

c

Oatmeal-Box Bug Cage

Now you can have a small insect zoo in your very own room. If you like catching insects, then you will want to make one or more bug cages. The cages are easy to construct and will hold many bugs or beetles. Add a little grass or a few leaves to the bottom of the cages, and don't keep any bug population too long! You wouldn't want to stay too long in a cage yourself. Remember to ask Mom if you can keep the bugs in your room. She may not like them as much as you.

Things You Need

1 oatmeal box
piece of screening, preferably plastic
pencil
scissors
yarn or cord
crayons or colored felt-tipped markers
poster paints

Let's Begin

1. Paint an empty oatmeal box a light color with poster paints.
2. Let the box dry.
3. Draw flower shapes on the box with a pencil.
4. Poke a hole in the center of each flower with a pencil, Fig. a.
**5. Put one blade of a pair of scissors into each hole, and cut out the flowers from the oatmeal box, Fig. b.
**6. Cut a piece of screening. Plastic is best. It should be as tall as the box and long enough to fit around the inside.
7. Roll the screening, and fit it into the box, Fig. c.
8. Poke a hole on both sides of the box near the top. Use a pencil.
9. Thread a long piece of cord or yarn through both holes.
10. Tie both ends together, Fig. d.
11. Pull the cord so you can put the cover on the box.
12. Draw leaves, a sun, or clouds on the box with crayons or colored felt-tipped markers. Don't forget to keep the lid on the box when bugs are inside.

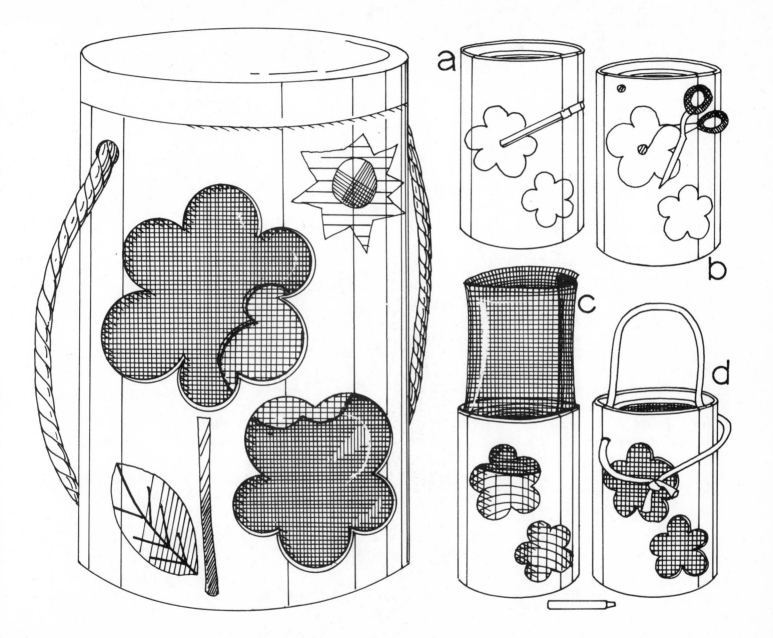

a

b

c

d

Coffee-Can Totem Pole

The Indians made totem poles to honor the gods they worshiped. To make them, they had first to find a very tall, very straight tree. The bark would be removed, and faces of animals and evil spirits carved into the wood. When it was finished, the totem pole was placed in the ground. It stood very tall. There were many totem poles in a village.

How would you like to have a totem pole? You don't really have to be an Indian to have one. Your totem pole will not be *very* big, but it is large enough for you to invite your fellow braves to your house. You can have a powwow by your totem pole every week.

Things You Need

coffee cans with lids
colored construction paper
tape
scissors
paper paste

Let's Begin

1. Wrap a piece of colored construction paper around each can, Fig. a.
2. Tape the paper together around the cans, Fig. b.
3. Trim away any extra paper that may go above and below the cans.
4. Cut out three feather shapes from colored construction paper. Paste them to the top of one of the cans, Fig. c.
5. Paste a long strip of paper to the back of that can. Glue feather shapes to this strip, Fig. d.
6. Cut out funny paper eyes, noses, mouths, and crazy war-paint shapes.
7. Using these, paste a face to each can.
8. Make the totem pole by putting one can on top of the other.
9. The more cans you make, the taller your totem pole will be.

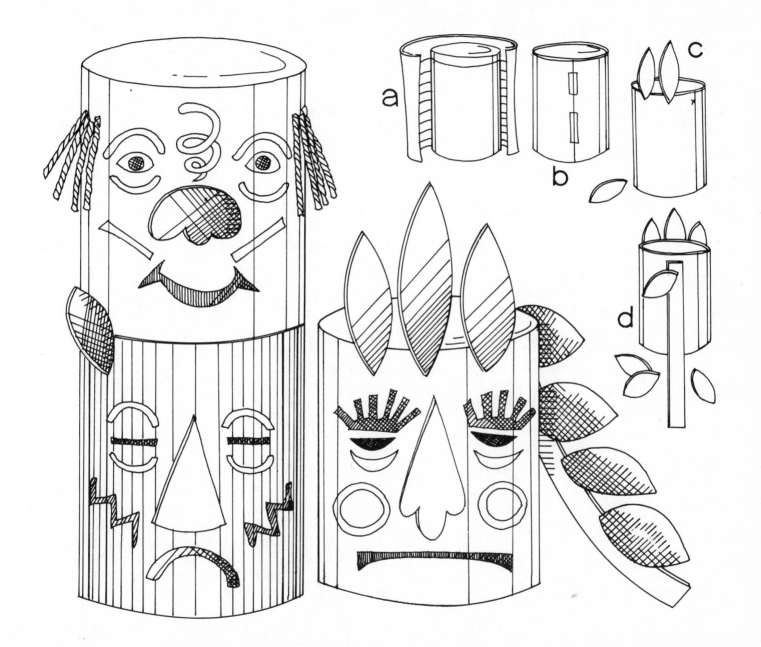

Paper-Plate Warrior Shield

If you were a Knight of the Round Table you would need two important things. The first would be your sword. It would have to be razor sharp. You would have to know how to use it to defend yourself. You would also need a shield. A shield would protect you from your enemy's strong sword flashing.

Today, swords and shields are no longer used. Most of them are in museums or hanging on a wall. You may not have a warrior's shield on your wall, but you can easily make one. This shield is not the one used by the knights of long ago, but somewhat like the kind the brave warriors of Africa still treasure.

Things You Need

1 large paper plate
colored construction paper
paper paste
tape or stapler
1 sheet of tracing paper
pencil
scissors

Let's Begin

1. Cut out design shapes from colored construction paper like the ones you see in the illustration.
2. Paste these shapes to the underside or bottom of a paper plate.
3. Make the handle for the shield from a paper strip cut a little longer than the size of the plate. Tape or staple it to the other side of the plate, Fig. a.
4. Trace the feather, Shape b, from the book onto a sheet of tracing paper.
5. Cut out the feather from the tracing paper.
6. Use the feather cutout to trace three feathers onto different-colored construction paper.
7. Cut out these feathers and paste to the bottom front of the shield.
8. Play with your shield by holding the handle on your arm or hang the shield on your wall as a decoration.

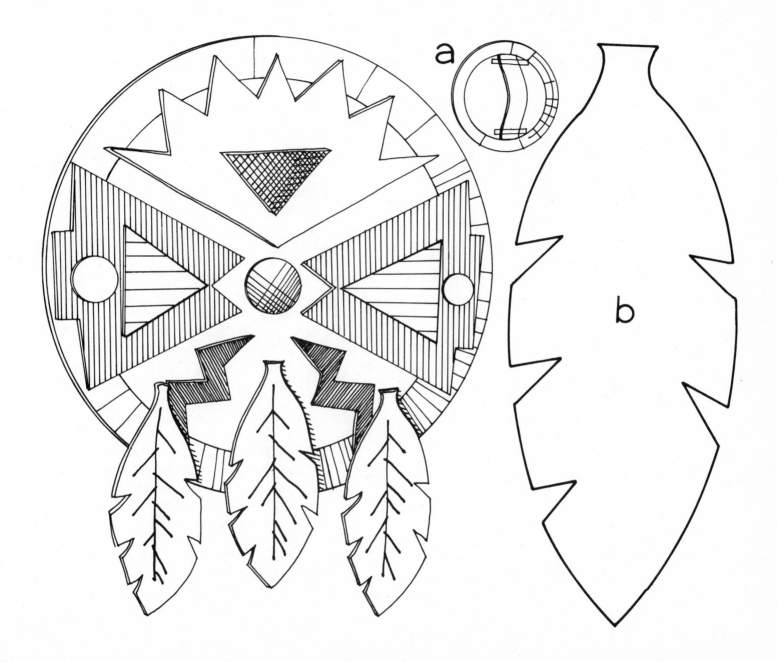

a

b

Milk-Carton Village

Some of the towns out West are small enough for one man to own. There are several houses, a grocery store, and maybe even a candy store. How would you like to own your own village? It's very possible. This is a very healthy town —the buildings are made from milk cartons. If you like to drink milk, then who knows? Your little village might develop into a large city.

Things You Need

milk cartons
colored construction paper
scissors
tape
paper paste
crayons or colored felt-tipped markers

Let's Begin

1. Cut a sheet of colored construction paper as tall as the carton is straight-sided.
2. Wrap the paper around the carton, Fig. a.
3. Tape the paper together around the carton, Fig. b.
4. Cut out window, door, flower box, and flower shapes from colored construction paper.
5. Paste the house decorations onto the carton.
6. Cut the roof from a piece of red or orange construction paper. It should be long enough to overhang the carton slightly when folded in half.
7. Make the stairs from a piece of construction paper by folding it back and forth, Fig. c. Paste stairs under the door.
8. Make the chimney from a construction-paper rectangle with a point at the bottom, Fig. b. Draw a brick design on it.
9. Cut a small slit on one side of the folded roof. It should be smaller than the point on the chimney.
10. Draw a roof design on both sides of the folded roof. Use crayons or colored felt-tipped markers.
11. Push the pointed end of the chimney shape into the slit in the roof.
12. Glue or tape the finished roof and chimney to the top of the carton, Fig. b.
13. Use cream or Half and Half containers for smaller houses. Decorate them the same way you did the big house.
14. Make a village for your trains or racing cars.

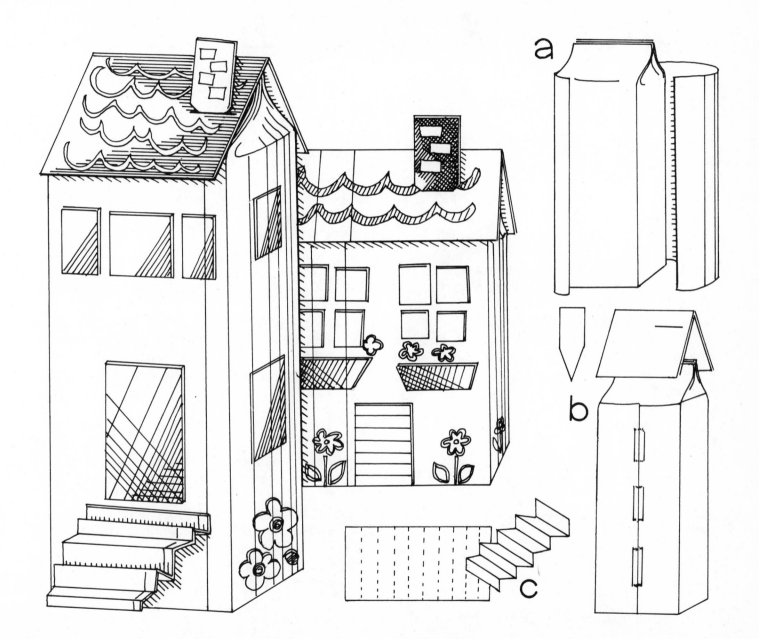

a

b

c

Soap-Box Wagon

You may not have a real red wagon but you can make a small one. Next time Mom finishes using a box of laundry detergent, ask her for it. With it, a fun pull wagon can be yours. It is not big enough for you to sit in it, but you can cart your toys in it.

Things You Need

1 large soap-powder box
tape
scissors
4 brass paper fasteners
cord or yarn
pencil
poster paints
paintbrush

Let's Begin

1. Tape the open end of the soap box closed, Fig. a.

**2. Cut away the front side of the box, Fig. a.

3. Use a pencil to punch two holes into each end on the long side of the box for the wheels, Fig. b.

4. Punch two holes close to each other on one of the short sides of the box for the pull cord, Fig. b.

5. Paint the box with red poster paint.

6. Use a large glass to draw four wheels on heavy cardboard. Cut out wheels.

7. Punch a hole through the center of each wheel with a sharp pencil.

8. Push a paper fastener through the wheels and through the holes punched in the long sides of the box, Fig. c.

9. Open the fastener prongs inside the box to keep the wheels on.

10. Tie a long length of yarn or cord through the two holes on the short side of the box.

11. Tie the cord in a knot.

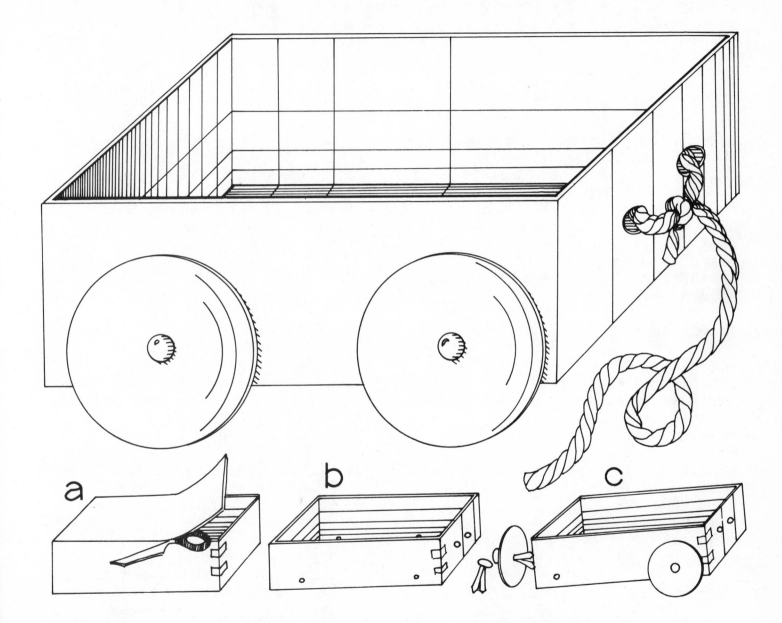

a

b

c

Odds-and-Ends Robot

Is it a creature from outer space or did a mad scientist make it?

Robots are machines that do the same things that people do. They walk and talk, though they are made of metal. *Your* robot will be made from things that are usually thrown away. Look around the house for the "junk" needed to build him. The odds and ends you use all together suddenly combine to make a wonderful mechanical man.

Things You Need

oatmeal box
tuna-fish can
2 cardboard tubes from inside rolls of paper towels
waxed-paper box
straw
2 beads
pencil
liquid white glue
poster paints
crayons or colored felt-tipped markers
watercolor brush

Let's Begin

**1. Remove the lid from a tuna-fish can.

2. Glue the can to the top of an oatmeal box, open side down, Fig. a.

**3. Cut one of the cardboard tubes in three equal parts.

4. Punch a hole with a sharp pencil completely through the center of one of the tube sections. You can use a paper punch.

5. Glue this tube to the top of the tuna fish can, Fig. b.

6. Push a straw through both holes of the tube, Fig. c.

7. Glue a bead to both ends of the straw, Fig. d.

8. Glue the other two sections of the cut tube to the oatmeal box, close to the top, Fig. e.

**9. Cut off one end of an empty waxed-paper box.

10. Glue the waxed-paper-box section to the front of the oatmeal box, Fig. f.

11. Cut the other cardboard tube into two equal parts.

12. Glue both parts of the tube to the bottom of the oatmeal box, Fig. g.

13. Paint the robot with grey poster paint.

14. Paint red circles on the tuna-fish can, and blue circles on the front box.

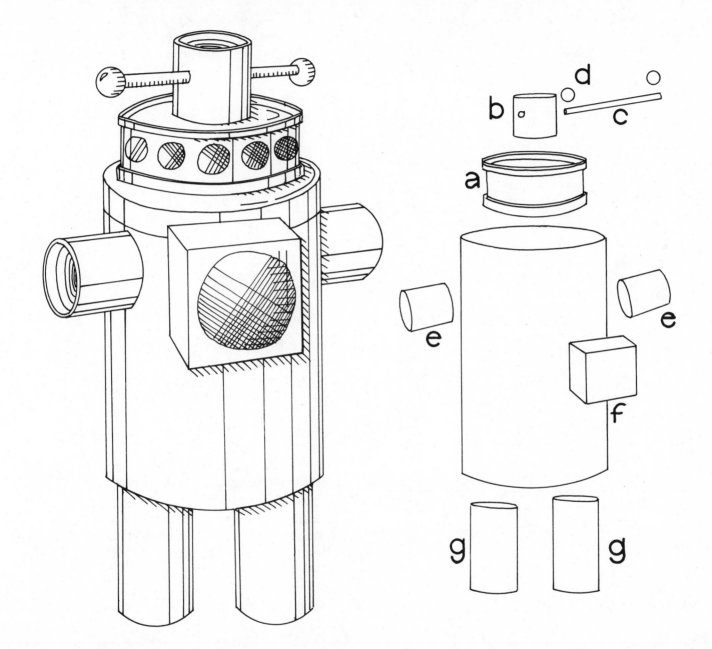

Sewing-Spool Telescope

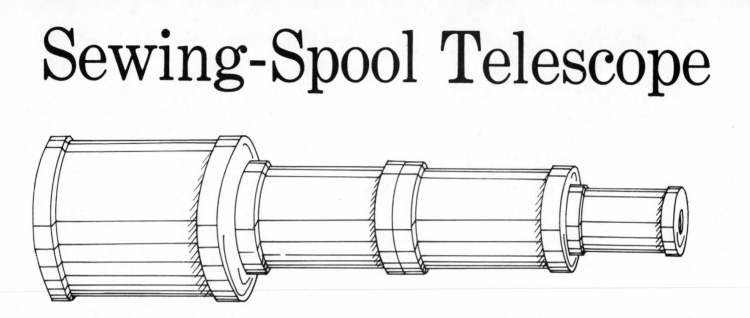

You have been sailing on the ocean for many days. There is blue all around you. Blue sky and blue ocean. Finally, the sailor in the crow's nest shouts the words you have wanted to hear. "Land, ahoy!" What is the first thing you are going to reach for? That's right. You take your telescope in your hand and place it to your weary eye. It's true. There is land ahead of you at last . . .

It's fun to imagine you are the captain of a sailing ship or maybe an evil pirate. With your sewing-spool telescope you can sail the high seas and always spot the land which lies just across the horizon.

Things You Need
sewing-thread spools of different sizes
1 drinking straw
liquid white glue
poster paints

watercolor brush

Let's Begin
1. Place the straw into the hole of a large sewing spool.
2. Put the spool on a piece of paper with the straw standing up.
3. Add a little liquid white glue to the top of this first spool.
4. Stack two or three medium-sized spools onto the straw, gluing them together with liquid white glue.
5. Glue a small spool on the straw last.
6. Remove the straw. Be careful not to move the spools. (If you keep the straw in the spools, trim when dry.)
7. Dry overnight.
8. Paint the telescope with poster paint.

My room
is a
special place

My room is a special place

Your home is a place where everyone in your family stays dry when it rains, eats food when he is hungry, and sleeps safely when he is tired. It is a comfortable place with a friendly kitchen and a cozy living room. Best of all, there is a room for you. It may not be as big as you'd like it to be, but it is your own special place.

Look around your room. Your Mom and Dad and you have made it a friendly place. There must be a picture or two of your favorite real or make-believe people. Toys are probably neatly placed all around (or are they?). There might even be an airplane hanging from the ceiling, or a pretty marionette dancing on the wall. Are you happy with the way your room is decorated? Although your imagination can turn it into a castle keep or an Old West city, maybe it could use some real-life embellishment.

Now is the time to decorate that bare ceiling or those colorless out-of-the-way places. In this chapter you will make things for many of the important parts of your room. There's a mobile for that ceiling, a carton to keep your toys in, even a braided fabric rug. How about a stained-glass window shade? Since only one room of your home is really yours, make it a place that you really love and don't want to leave unless you have to.

Collage a Special Container

There must be hundreds of paper objects around your home—from your old report cards to postage stamps. Any object made of paper can be used in this collage project. If you remember, a collage is lots of paper things pasted together to make a picture or to decorate an object. Pick out your favorite pictures, greeting cards, or any paper scraps. Then find tin cans, boxes, or even a waste-paper basket—you can collage almost anything. With a little glue, you can then turn these objects into lovely things for your room. You might even want to make a present for someone special in your family.

Things You Need

greeting cards, stamps, pieces of fabric, magazine cutouts, invitations, food labels, etc.
colored construction paper
paper paste
liquid white glue
crayons or colored felt-tipped markers
waste-paper basket
coffee can with plastic lid
large box
small paintbrush
paper cup

Let's Begin

1. Paste the special things you have collected onto a waste-paper basket, coffee can, or a large box. Paste each piece close together so that no part of the basket, can, or box shows. Cover the entire container with pictures.
2. If you want to make a special can or box, write the name of what is to be put in it on a piece of colored construction paper.
3. Glue the name on the container.
4. Pour liquid white glue into a paper cup.
5. Brush glue over all of the pictures.
6. Let the glue dry overnight.
7. The next day, brush another coating of glue over the pictures.
8. Let the second coating dry completely.
9. Glue and dry at least two more times.
10. When making the box, you might cover the entire box or just the lid.

Pillow-Case Pajama Bag

Before you start your evening fun, you usually want to get comfortable. You can't wait to take off the clothes you've been in all day. What could be more cozy than your pajamas. Now let's see! Where did you put them? They are probably in a dresser drawer. Or hanging in your closet. Maybe Mom put them on your bed. Since they are so special and personal, why not make a home just for them—somewhere you'll know they'll always be? With the Pillow-Case Pajama Bag, you will never have a problem finding them. Your pajamas will be behind your door waiting for you every night.

Things You Need

plain pillow case
small curtain rod
scissors
indelible felt-tipped markers

Let's Begin

**1. Cut six evenly spaced slits on one top edge of a pillow case, Fig. a.
2. Draw the design on the other side of the case with indelible felt-tipped markers (see book).
3. Draw the Letter A with a red apple next to it.
4. Draw the Letter B with a yellow banana next to it.
5. Draw the Letter C with an orange carrot next to it.
6. Draw green leaves on the apple and the carrot.
7. Push both ends of a curtain rod, from opposite sides, in and out of the slits, Fig. b.
**8. Fit the rods together to the size of the pillow case.
**9. Attach the pajama bag to the back of your closet door.

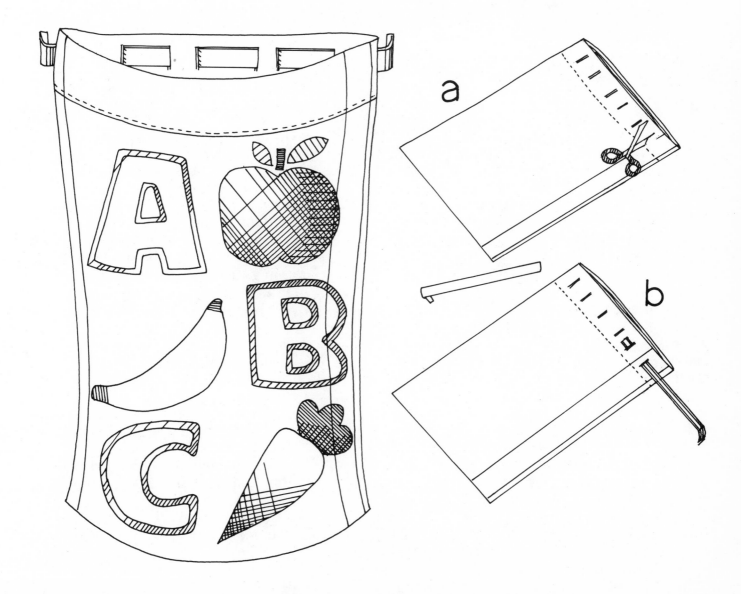

a

b

Drinking-Straw Mobile

The ancient sailors used stars to guide them across the ocean. It is difficult to see stars, much less be a navigator, in your bedroom. What about a star mobile, then? With it, a galaxy of stars will orbit inside your room. They will lead you to whatever shores you wish to dream . . .

Things You Need

4 drinking straws
1 sheet of tracing paper
pencil
scissors
colored construction paper
needle and thread
1 small two-hole button

Let's Begin

1. Trace the bottom star (with the circle on it) from the book onto a sheet of tracing paper.
2. Cut out the star.
3. Use the cutout star to trace nine stars onto yellow or blue construction paper.
4. Cut out the nine stars.
**5. Thread a needle, knot the thread, and sew through one point of a star. Now sew the star to one end of one of the straws, Fig. b, leaving enough thread between star and straw to allow star to dangle. Knot thread around straw. Repeat this operation for eight of the stars. Every straw should have two stars dangling from it, one at each end.
6. Place the four straws on top of each other. Form an evenly spaced star by crossing the straws at their centers, Fig. a.
7. Crush the straws with your finger at the place they meet.
8. Thread a needle with a long length of thread.
9. Sew down through the centers of the straws.
10. Pass the needle through one hole of the button placed underneath the juncture of the straws.
11. Sew up through the other hole of the button and back through the center of the straws.
12. Knot the thread.
13. Sew the last star through the center of the mobile.
14. Hang the mobile from the ceiling with tape.

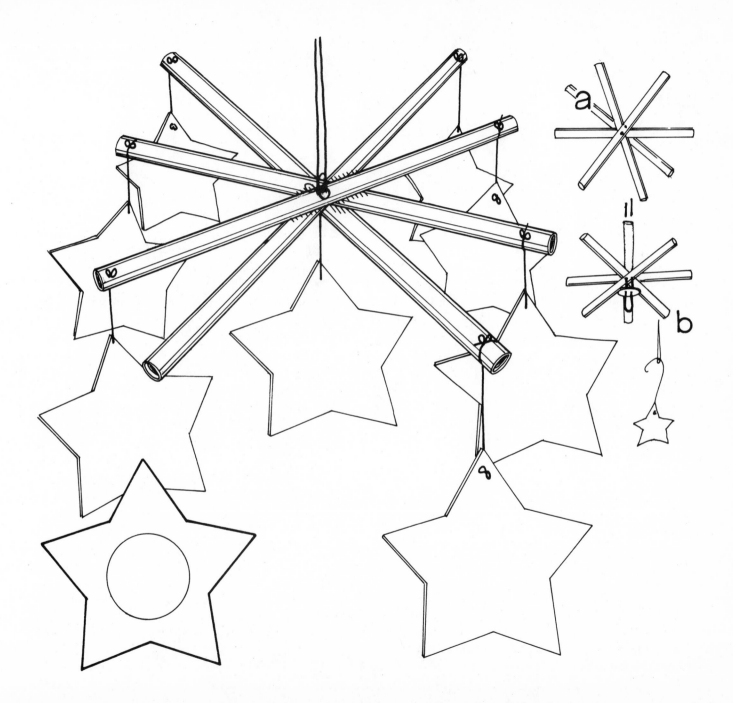

a

b

Stacked Carton Toy Box

Your toys are very special. When you are finished playing with them, why not put them in a safe place? Build a toy box; in fact, build an apartment house of toy boxes. Stack one toy box on top of another. Mom will be very happy. She likes to see your toys put neatly away.

Things You Need

3 same-sized sturdy cardboard cartons with lids intact
large sheets of colored construction paper
tape
paper paste
scissors

Let's Begin

1. For small boxes, tape colored construction paper to the box. The paper should be cut to the same size as the sides of the box, Fig. a. For large boxes, paint the box a bright color with poster paint or paint you can borrow from your dad. Paper or paint each box a different color.

2. Make the triangular covers for the corners of the box from small yellow squares of construction paper cut from corner to corner, Fig. b.
3. Paste a triangle to each corner of each box, Fig. c.
4. Cut the letters that spell TOY and BOX from square pieces of colored construction paper. Use the letter drawings in the book as a guide.
5. Cut two of each letter except the letter O. Cut four O's.
6. Stack the boxes and paste on the letters T O Y, one letter to one side of each of the boxes. The boxes should be arranged so that T is on the top box, O is on the middle box, and Y is on the bottom box.
7. On the next sides of the boxes, paste the letters B O X, top to bottom.
8. On the next sides of the boxes, paste the letters T O Y, top to bottom, as before.
9. On the last sides, paste the letters B O X.
10. Fill the boxes with toys. Try scrambling and unscrambling the letters by stacking the boxes in different combinations.

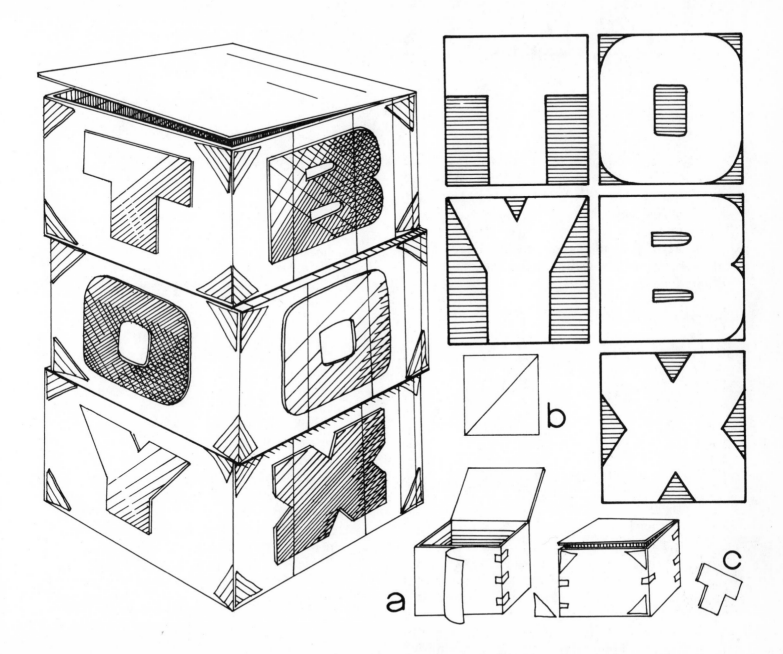

A Braided Fabric Rug

Little girls like to braid their hair. It makes them look so very cute. Hair isn't the only thing you can braid. A warm and cozy rug starts as the longest braid you have ever seen. This rug will be pretty because it has many colors. All of your old favorite worn-out clothes can become a braided-rug foot warmer for chilly mornings.

Things You Need

strips of colored fabric
needle with a large eye
heavy thread
scissors

Let's Begin

**1. Cut strips of fabric from old clothes or from new fabric that is bought in the store.

2. Cut each strip no wider than the two lines between which the arrows are pointing (see guide in book). Make each strip as long as you want.

3. Tie three strips together in a knot, Fig. a.

4. To braid strips, start by folding strip Number 1 over strip Number 2, the middle strip, Fig. b. After you have done this you will notice that strip Number 1 is now in the middle.

5. Fold strip Number 3 over the new middle strip, Number 1, Fig. c. After you have done this you will notice that strip Number 3 is now in the middle.

6. Now, strip Number 2 goes over the new middle strip, Number 3, Fig. d. What you are doing is always putting the right strip over the middle strip and then the left strip over the middle strip.

7. When the strips start to get short, sew a new strip onto each with a needle and thread, Fig. e.

8. Start making the rug by rolling the braid around the knot you made when you tied the strips together, Fig. f.

9. Sew the braid to itself in a circle as you roll the braid around the center knot. Sew and braid as you go, adding new strips to the three main strips as you need them, Fig. g.

10. When the rug is the size you want, tie the ends of the three strips into a knot.

11. Tuck the knot and a little bit of the braid into the underside of the rug.

12. Sew the knot to the underside of the rug.

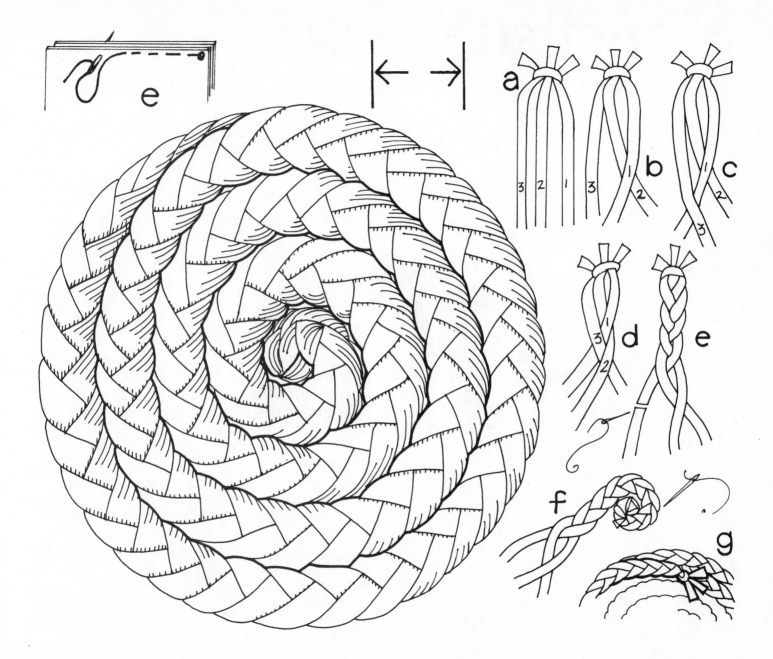

Stenciled Curtains

The curtains on your bedroom windows make your room a cheerful place. If you want to brighten your room even more than it is now, why not stencil designs on the window curtains? You can buy stencils in the store, or you can make them yourself, as we will do here. The circle and diamond shapes will brighten up old or new curtains. After you've practiced a little, why not make up your own stencil shapes and patterns?

Things You Need

plain window curtains
piece of cardboard
pencil
scissors
indelible felt-tipped markers
tracing paper

Let's Begin

**1. Remove your curtains and wash them.
  2. Trace the diamond and circle designs from the book onto a sheet of tracing paper.

3. Rub a pencil on the back of the tracing paper, covering the lines from below.
4. Place the tracing on a piece of cardboard with the drawing facing up.
5. Retrace the lines of the circle and the diamond, pressing hard on the paper, Fig. a. The designs will appear on the cardboard when you lift up the tracing paper.
6. Poke a hole in the center of the cardboard diamond and circle, Fig. b.
**7. Put your scissors into the hole and begin to cut out each shape along the pencil lines on the cardboard, Fig. c.
8. Place the cardboard stencils near the bottom of your curtain and close to one side. You can arrange the stencil so that the circle is over or under the diamond.
9. Ink in all the fabric that shows through the cutout diamond and circle with an indelible felt-tipped marker, Fig. d.
10. Make as many designs as you can fit across the bottom of the curtain.
**11. Hang the curtains on your window.

154

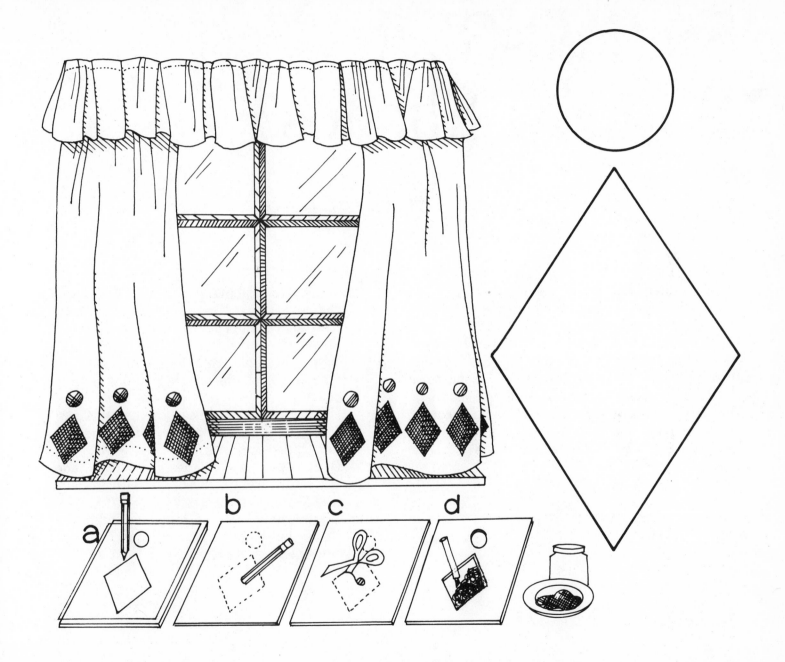

a b c d

Stained-Glass Window Shades

Does the morning sun, peeping around your window shade, awake you? Maybe it would help if the shade was prettier. What you can do is stencil designs on it. The stenciled fish design will make it seem like you are waking up under the ocean or in a small submarine. The light of the morning sun will paint a beautiful picture as it tries to come through your window shade. You won't mind so much getting up in the morning.

Things You Need

1 white paper shade
1 sheet of tracing paper
pencil
scissors
indelible felt-tipped markers

Let's Begin

1. Trace the fish design from the book onto a sheet of tracing paper and, following the directions for the preceding craft, cut out a stencil from cardboard.
**2. When you have made your stencil, take down the shade from your window.
3. Unroll the shade and lay it flat on the floor.
4. Using the stencil, ink in the fish and tail design on the cardboard with the indelible felt-tipped markers.
5. Draw eyes and tail designs onto shade with different-colored indelible felt-tipped markers.
6. Draw green seaweed and blue bubbles.
**7. Hang the shade on your window, and see how the fish glisten.

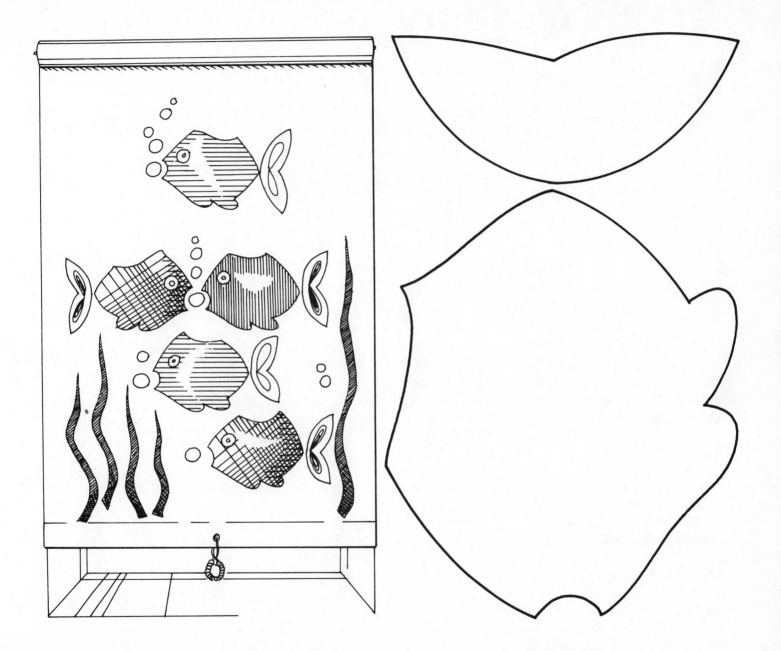

Mirror Decals

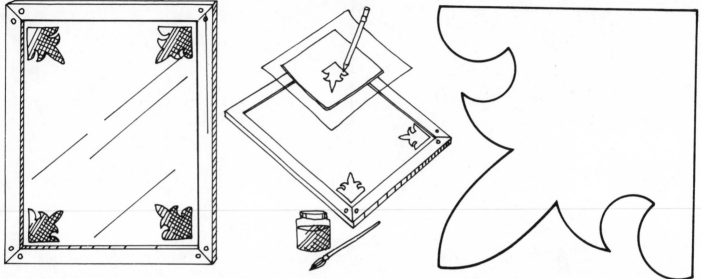

"Mirror, mirror, on the wall . . ." Are you the fairest one of all? Of course you are. Look in the mirror and see yourself. You look fine, but what about the mirror? What your room needs is a special decaled mirror. Every time you look in it, your face will be surrounded by pretty decal designs. With some waxed paper and paint, your decal mirror will be the best-looking of them all.

Things You Need

1 mirror in a frame
1 sheet of tracing paper
pencil
piece of waxed paper
poster paints   paper cup
kitchen cleanser   watercolor brush

Let's Begin

1. Trace the design from the book onto a sheet of tracing paper.
2. Put a sheet of waxed paper over one corner of the mirror.
3. Place the tracing paper over the waxed paper. The corner of the design should be fitted into the corner of the mirror.
4. Draw over your pencil lines with a pencil.
5. When you lift up both pieces of paper you will see the design drawn in wax on the mirror.
6. Repeat the procedure for all four corners.
7. Mix your colored paint with a little bit of kitchen cleanser in a paper cup.
8. Paint in each design.

What shall
I wear?

What shall I wear?

Your clothes are the closest things to you. They keep you warm when it's cool, cool when it's warm, and make you look the way you want to look every minute of the day. You are rather lucky. When your clothes wear out, your Mom goes shopping at the clothing store. Just imagine if you were a person living in a cave many millions of years ago. You would have to hunt for your clothing. Cloth was not yet invented and primitive man used animal skins to make his wardrobe. This was good for the cave man. Besides getting a new suit he also ate a delicious supper.

It wasn't easy making clothing, even if you had a deer or bear hide. The skin had to be treated so that it was soft enough to wear. The Eskimos in Alaska used and still use sealskin hides to make boots, gloves, and heavy coats. If you lived in Alaska, you would need heavy fur clothing to protect you from the cold weather. In other primitive parts of the world, making clothing is one of the chores people have to do in order to stay alive.

It's a little easier for you today—still, there are a few items of clothing you probably don't have but have always wanted. Headbands, string belts, love beads, and many more. With your hands, a snip of the scissors, and a needle and thread, you can be on your way to a world of fun fashions. You thought you were good-looking? Wait until you finish making all of the items of clothing on the following pages. You are going to be the best-dressed person on your street. Your friends might even ask you to make something for them.

Tie-Dye Tee Shirt

Everyone is wearing wild tee shirts. These crazy shirts have all kinds of designs and different sayings on them. Don't be seen without one. Make your own tie-dye tee shirt. All it takes is string and some dyes. You can design many beautiful patterns and have a sunburst of exciting colors. Your tee shirt will be extra special because there won't be anyone in your neighborhood with one like yours. The great thing about tie-dyeing is that no two designs look the same. Once you get started, you'll want all of your clothes to be colored that way.

Things You Need

1 light-colored tee shirt
boxed dyes of various colors
elastic bands or string
small bowl.

Let's Begin

1. Gather a section of the tee shirt and tie it with an elastic band or with strong string. Make a very tight knot, Fig. a.

2. Tie a second knot halfway down from the first, Fig. b. Repeat this procedure, gathering and knotting material in various places all over the shirt.
3. In some gathers, but not all, tie a third knot halfway down from the second knot, Fig. c.
4. Pour yellow or another light color of boxed dye into a small bowl. Mix with a small amount of water.
5. Dip the entire shirt into the dye. Ring out.
6. Pour light green, or another medium shade of boxed dye into a small bowl. Mix with a small amount of water.
7. Dip all of the gathers into the dye, this time only as far as the middle knot, Fig. d.
8. Add blue, or another dark color of boxed dye to a small bowl. Mix with a small amount of water.
9. Where gathers make three knots, dip into dye, dyeing the last section only.
10. Let the tee shirt dry without removing any of the knots.
11. When dry, remove the elastic bands or tied string.

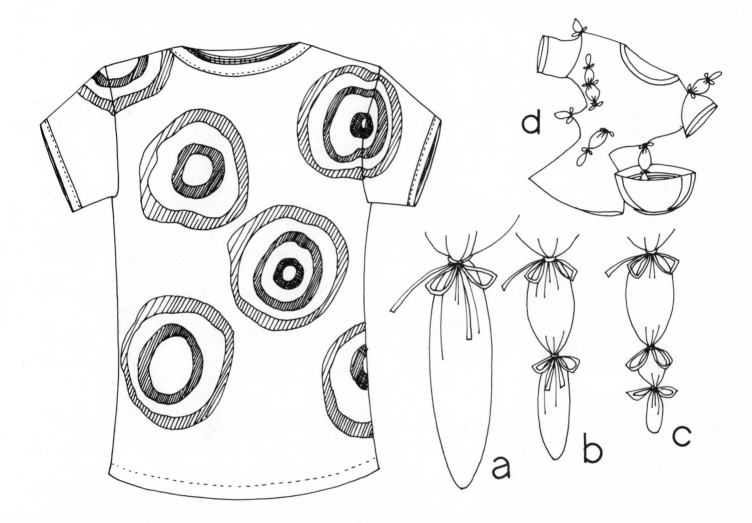

a b c d

Crayon-Batik a Scarf

Did you ever wonder how designs are put on fabric? Most designs are printed just the way a newspaper is printed. Long before printing machines were invented, though, clothing had designs and patterns. One of the ways this was done was by batiking the fabric. When you batik a piece of fabric you start with a light, solid-colored piece of material. With wax and dyes, the batiking process adds colorful designs to the fabric. You will not be using wax and dyes the way people did hundreds of years ago. Crayons will do just as well. Your batik scarf will look absolutely lovely on your head.

Things You Need

white silk scarf
crayons
boxed dyes of various colors
bowl
clothing iron
paper toweling

Let's Begin

1. Place the corners of the scarf on the heart, diamond, and circle design on the bottom right of the scarf illustration in the book. Trace onto the scarf with a pencil.
2. Color in all the hearts on the scarf with a heavy coating of red crayon, Fig. a.
3. Place each corner between two sheets of paper toweling.
**4. Use a medium-hot clothes iron to iron each heart so that all of the wax melts into the silk, Fig. b.
5. Mix a light-color dye into a small bowl with water.
6. Dip the entire scarf into the dye, Fig. c.
7. Let the scarf dry completely.
8. When the scarf is dry, color in all the diamond shapes on the scarf with a heavy coating of green crayon, Fig. d.
**9. Iron the diamonds the same way you ironed the hearts.
10. Dip the scarf into a medium-dark dye solution.
11. Let the scarf dry completely.
12. When the scarf has dried, color in all the circles on the scarf with a heavy coating of blue crayon, Fig. e.
**13. Iron the circles the same way you ironed the hearts and diamonds.
**14. Iron the whole scarf before you wear it.

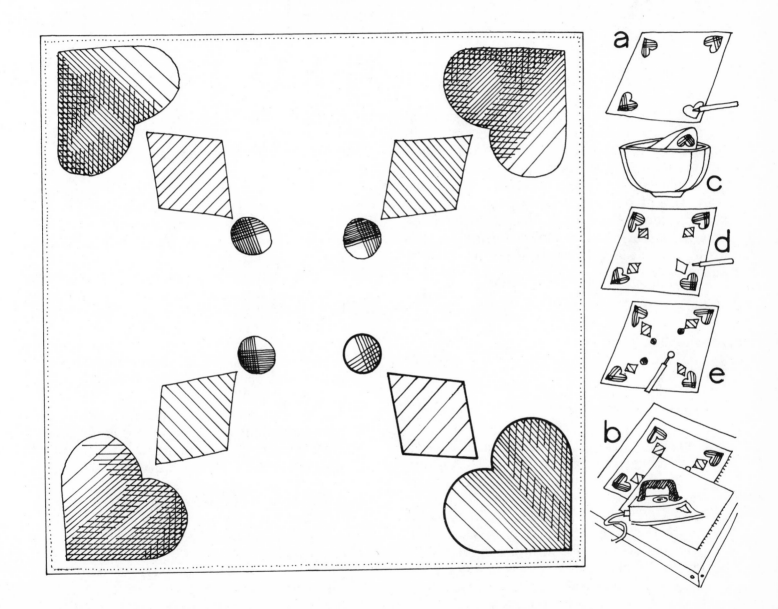

Macramé a Belt

If you like to dress in the latest funky fashions, then you will need a macramé belt. Most belts are made from leather. The belt you are going to make is made of yarn or heavy cord tied into interesting knots. The knots were invented by sailors during their long voyages across the sea, and the process is called macramé. You need only two things for this project: a piece of yarn or cord and a lot of patience.

Things You Need

yarn or heavy cord

Let's Begin

GENERAL INSTRUCTIONS

1. You will work with four strands of cord. To more easily depict the knots, each group of two strands is shown in the drawings as one.
2. The single-headed arrow will always indicate the right two strands. When tied, they will always return to the right side.
3. The double-headed arrow will always indicate the left two strands. When tied, they will always return to the left side.

TO MACRAMÉ

1. Fold two very long lengths of yarn or cord in half, Fig. a.
2. Tie both lengths of cord at the loop tops, Fig. b.
3. Start by bringing the right cords (single-headed arrow) over the left cords (double-headed arrow), Fig. c.
4. Form a loop on the right side, Fig. c.
5. Bring the single-headed arrow cords behind the double-headed arrow cords, and then through the loop on the right, Figs. d and e.
6. Next bring the left or double-headed arrow cords over the right or single-headed arrow cords, Fig. f.
7. Form a loop on the left side.
8. Bring the double-headed arrow cords behind the single-headed arrow cords, and then through the loop on the left side, Figs. g and h.
9. Continue to tie these knots going from the right and then to the left.
10. When you are near the end, make a knot in the belt.
11. Tie a different color of yarn or cord to both ends of the belt. Use these to fasten the belt around your waist.

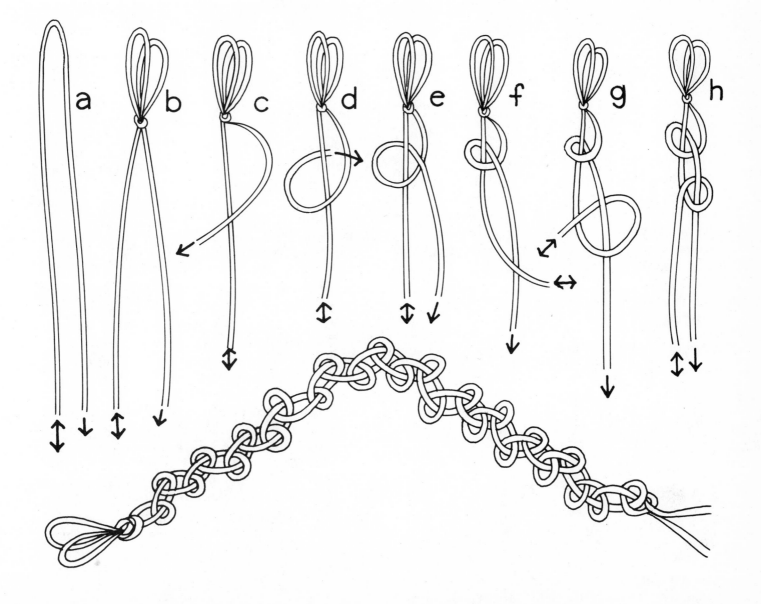

Ball-Fringe Apron

Do you like to help Mom in the kitchen? If you do, then you probably wear an apron. Aprons are important because they keep your clothes from getting soiled and messy. If your Mom lets you do some of the cooking, why not make yourself an apron? After you make the first one for yourself, surprise Mom and give her one.

Things You Need

washable fabric
ribbon
ball fringe
needle and thread
scissors

Let's Begin

1. Choose a piece of fabric that is wide enough to fit completely around your waist. You can make it as long as you want.
2. Fold a little of the side edges of the fabric over and sew down with a simple running stitch. **To do the running stitch,** first thread the needle and knot the thread. Sew over and under through the fabric, making stitches a little distant from each other. (Figs. a and b.)
3. Sew a running stitch along the top side of the fabric, and a little bit down from the top edge, Fig. b.
4. Pull the thread until the fabric begins to gather.
5. Gather the fabric enough to fit across the front of your waist, Fig. c.
6. Knot the thread several times before you cut away the excess.
7. Turn the apron around.
8. Cut a piece of ribbon long enough to fit around your waist two times, Fig. d.
9. Sew the center of the ribbon over the stitches that formed the gathers, Fig. e.
10. Sew several "tacking down" stitches on the end before you cut off the thread.
11. Turn the apron around and sew a bottom hem, folding the fabric over onto the back side of the apron, Fig. f.
12. Sew a length of ball fringe across the bottom edge of the front of the apron.

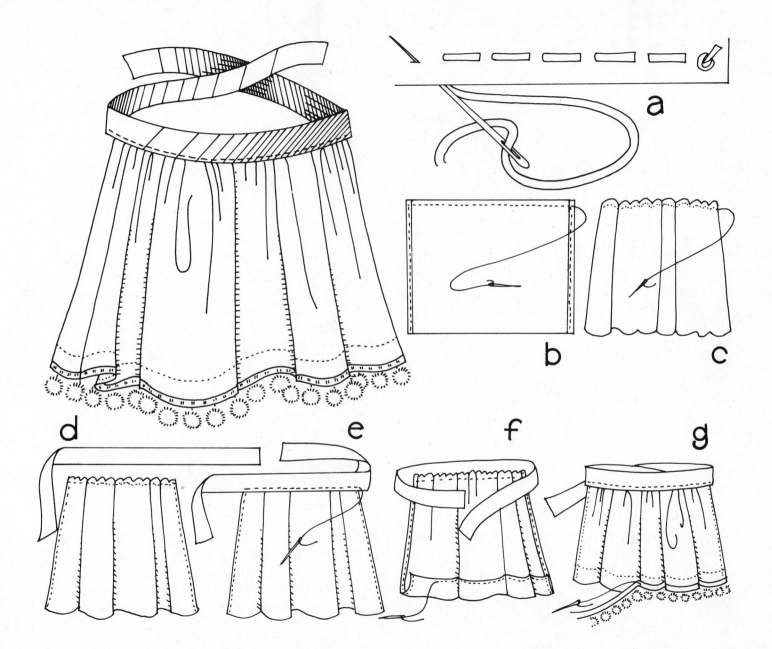

a

b

c

d

e

f

g

String a Necklace

Necklaces are beautiful because of the wonderful things they string together. Seashells, wooden beads, and pearls are some of the popular necklace items. Most of the beads and shapes for these decorative necklaces are in your home, and are very easy to make.

Things You Need

colored construction paper
tracing paper
tube macaroni
drinking straws
string
yarn
pencil
paper paste
scissors

Let's Begin

PAPER BEADS

1. Trace the triangle, Shape a, from the book onto a sheet of tracing paper.
2. Cut out the tracing and, using it as a pattern, trace the triangle onto colored construction paper as many times as you want beads for your necklace.
3. Cut out the triangles.
4. Cover one side of each triangle with paste.
5. Starting at the wide side of the triangle, roll it around a straw with the pasted side on the inside.
6. Press all of the edges down.
7. Roll all of the triangles on the straw, or on others if you need them.
8. When the beads have dried, cut off the straw at the edges of each bead, string the beads, and knot the ends of the string together, Fig. a.

MACARONI BEADS

1. String different sizes of tube macaroni, Fig. b, on yarn or string. Knot ends of string together.
2. Color macaroni with colored felt-tipped markers.

STRAW BEADS

1. Cut drinking straws on an angle with a pair of scissors, Fig. c.
2. String the straws on yarn or string. Knot the ends of string together. Color straws with colored felt-tipped markers.

PAPER SHAPE CHARMS

1. Cut different kinds of shapes from colored construction paper, like the ones shown in the illustration (Fig. d).
2. Poke a hole in the center of each shape. Use a sharp pencil.
3. String the charms on colored yarn. Tie string ends together and wear.

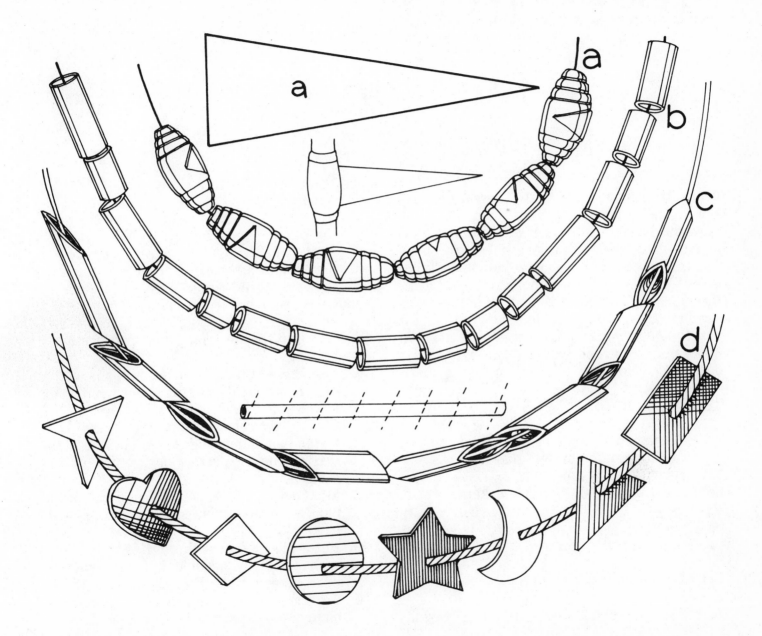

a

a

b

c

d

Headbands

When you think of headbands, the Indians probably come to mind first. There were very few Indians who didn't wear them. The long, straight, black braided hair of the Indian men and women was tucked neatly behind them. Today, many young people are beautifying *their* foreheads with headbands. It adds a little color to the top part of a person's body. The headband you are going to make will look just like the ones worn by the Indians. After you make your first one, you will probably start designing your own.

Things You Need

colored construction paper or colored felt
liquid white glue or brown glue
1 sheet of tracing paper
pencil or colored felt-tipped markers
scissors
paper punch
two lengths of yarn or cord

Let's Begin

1. Trace either headband and its designs from the book onto a sheet of tracing paper.
2. Cut out the headband shape from the tracing paper.
3. Trace this shape onto colored construction paper with a pencil. If you are using felt, use colored felt-tipped markers.
4. Cut out the headband shape from your paper or felt.
5. Cut out the designs from the headband tracing.
6. Use these cutouts to trace the shapes on paper or felt, depending upon what your headband is made of.
7. Cut out the colored shapes, and glue them to the headband, Fig. a. Follow the illustration for the correct positioning of the designs.
8. Make two holes on both sides of the headband with a paper punch or a sharp pencil, Fig. b.
9. Put a piece of yarn through both holes on each side of the headband. Tie the yarn to itself on each side, Fig. c.
10. Tie the yarn ends together to fasten the band around your head.

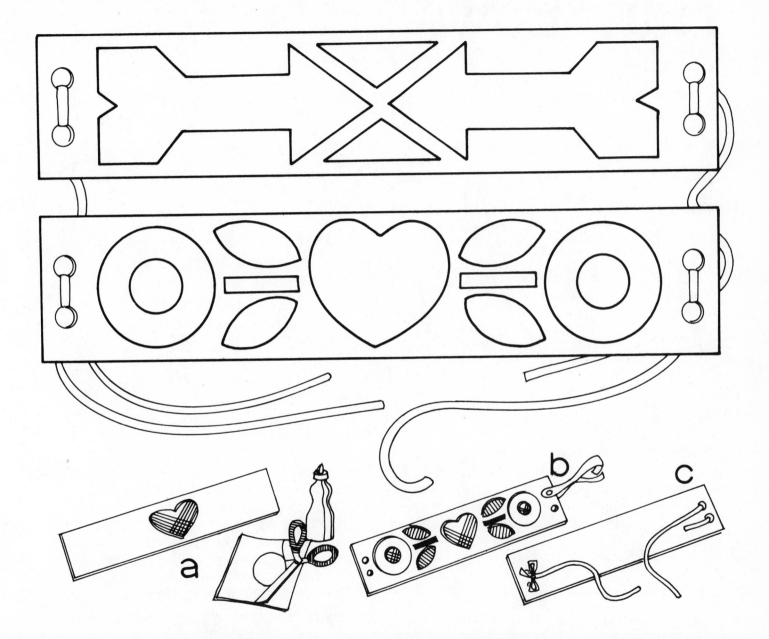

a

b

c

Hair Bows

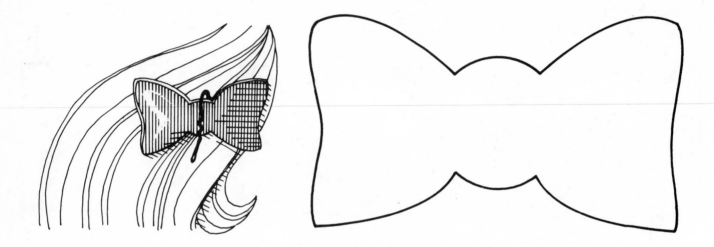

Are you the type of little girl who likes to put things in her hair when she wants to look pretty? Headbands, barrettes, and clips are good for holding your hair in place. What if you want just a little decoration in your hair? Do it with these pretty hair bows. Make a collection of all sizes and shapes.

Things You Need

1 sheet of tracing paper
pencil
scissors
colored construction paper or felt
bobby pin

Let's Begin

1. Trace the bow from the book onto a sheet of tracing paper.
2. Cut out the tracing and, using it as a pattern, trace the bow on a sheet of colored construction paper or scrap felt.
3. Cut out the paper or felt bow.
4. Attach it to your hair with a bobby pin.

Special crafts
for
special gifts

Special crafts for special gifts

You have many friends. Your two best friends are your Mom and Dad. They have loved and cared for you long before you can remember. The other members of your family come next. Your younger sister or older brother are perhaps among the best friends you will ever have. Then, of course, there's your pet. Even though he can't talk, he still likes being with you. He is a good and loyal friend.

When you leave your home, there is always a friend to greet you. Walking to school together, sitting in the same class, or playing outside—your pal is fun to be with. Do you like your teachers? Although they don't play with you they are frequently friends. Aunts, uncles, Grandmother, and Grandfather are other friends. How many times have they given you presents when they came to visit the family?

If you ever want to say "I love you" to one of your friends, there are several ways to do it. The best way is to say it, simply, and give the person a big hug or kiss. The second way is to give a beautiful gift. Gifts can be bought in the stores, but the best ones you can give are the ones you make all by yourself. Everyone loves a homemade gift. In this chapter there are many pretty gifts to make. Look at a calendar and see if someone special in your family is going to have a birthday soon. Maybe Mother's Day or Father's Day is coming. You don't really have to wait for a special day, though. A handmade present from you will be accepted anytime.

Appliquéd Wall Organizer

To appliqué means to sew one piece of fabric on top of another larger piece. If you have some empty wall space, why not make this pretty appliquéd wall organizer? Bobby pins, hair clips, bows—almost any small object can then find a home on your wall.

Things You Need

colored felt
curtain rod
embroidery thread
needle with a wide eye
tracing paper
safety pins
cotton stuffing or soft tissues
liquid white glue

Let's Begin

PRELIMINARIES
1. There are lettered shapes and lettered figures. Trace all of the letter shapes from the book onto tracing paper. Include all inner dotted-line designs where they appear. Trace two extra circles, Shape a or h. These will be used to make the snail and the lollipop.
2. Cut four pockets from the felt. Use the heavily outlined form in the illustration as a guide to the correct size.
3. Cut a large backing piece out of the felt. It should be big enough for the four pockets to fit comfortably on it, leaving a good margin of felt at the top (see illustration).
4. Sew a hem on top of the backing using a running stitch (to do this stitch see Ball-Fringe Apron, page 168). The hem should be large enough to allow a curtain rod to fit through it, Fig. a.

To Make the Pockets

THE FLOWER
1. Cut out Shape a from your tracing paper.
2. Pin the tracing on a piece of felt, and using it as a pattern, cut out the circle. Do not remove the tracing from the felt.
3. Hold a thin layer of cotton stuffing or two sheets of facial tissue behind the circle.
4. Trim the cotton or tissue a little smaller than the circle.
5. Pin the circle in the center of one of the felt pockets, keeping the cotton stuffing sandwiched in the middle.
**6. Thread a needle with embroidery thread.
7. Sew the circle with its tracing to the

178

(continued on page 180)

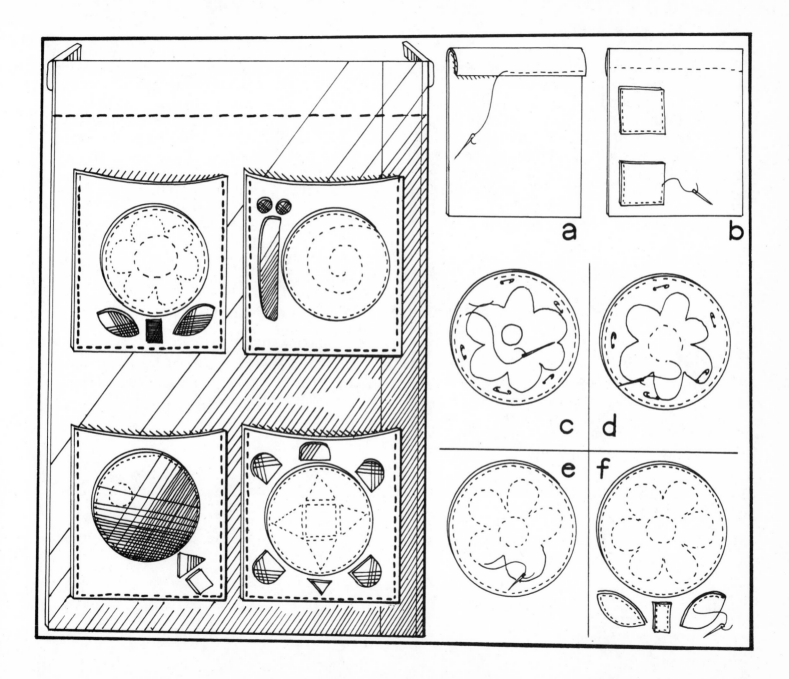

a

b

c

d

e

f

pocket around the outline of the circle, Fig. c. Use a running stitch.

8. Sew around the outline of the center circle design, Fig. d.
9. Sew around the petal outline, Fig. e.
10. Pull away the tissue. Cut out Shape c and Shape b from the tracing paper, and use them to cut out the shapes from the felt.
11. Sew the felt stem (Shape b) and leaf (Shape c) beneath the flower, Fig. f. Your flower is now complete.

THE SNAIL

1. Cut out one of the extra circles you drew on tracing paper.
2. Draw a spiral line on the tracing starting from the outer edge and curling into the middle.
3. The snail's body is Shape d and his antenna is Shape e. Following the procedure outlined for the flower, appliqué shapes to a pocket. Sew along inner swirl outline. See large illustration for a guide to the placement of body and antenna shapes.

THE LOLLIPOP

1. Cut out the other extra circle you drew from the tracing paper.
2. Draw a small inner circle on the tracing.
3. The lollipop stick is composed of Shapes f and g. Appliqué shapes to a felt pocket as above. See illustration for shape placement.

THE TURTLE

1. The turtle's shell is Shape h. His head and arms are Shape j, and his tail is Shape i. Follow procedures outlined above for appliquéing turtle shapes to the last felt pocket. Don't forget to sew along inner design of Shape h.

To Finish the Project

**1. Pin all pockets to the felt backing, Fig. b.
2. Sew pockets to backing using the running stitch. Sew along bottom and sides of pockets only, of course.

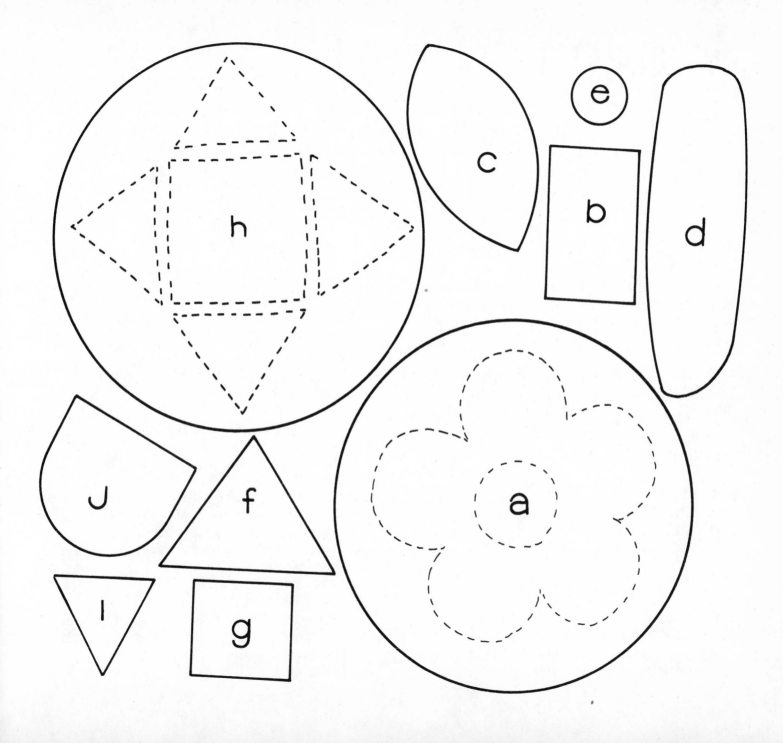

Woven Wall Hanging

When you get a hole in your socks, your mother darns it. That is, she weaves a patch with interlacing stitches. What she does is similar to what a weaver does when he is making cloth. In the old days, cloth was made on a loom. Today it is made by machine. Instead of weaving thread to make this wall hanging you will be removing them. The hanging you make will look attractive almost anywhere you put it.

Things You Need

piece of burlap fabric
ribbon, yarn, or colored string
curtain rod
needle and thread

Let's Begin

1. Fold over a little of the top edge of a piece of burlap and sew it down with a needle and thread. This is the hem into which you will later insert a curtain rod, Fig. a. Use a running stitch (see Ball-Fringe Apron, p. 168, for instructions on how to do it).
2. "Weave" the hanging by carefully pulling out threads from the burlap fabric. Start by pulling about ten threads from the bottom and the sides (horizontal and vertical threads) of the burlap (see arrows, Fig. b). The vertical threads will pull out only as far as the hem on the top because of the stitches you made to sew the hem. Cut the vertical threads away when they reach these stitches.
3. On the right side, pull away threads at different places so that you have solid spaces and open spaces, Fig. c.
4. Pinch several threads together in the open places, and tie them with ribbons, yarn, or colored string. Tie as many as you wish, Fig. d.
5. Slip a curtain rod through the top hem and adjust it to the size of the wall hanging.
**6. Hang on a wall or door.

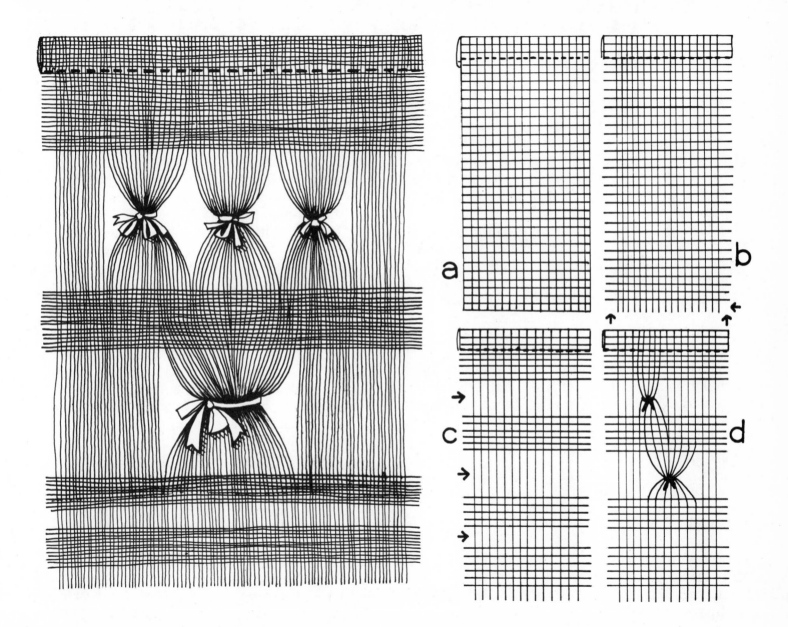

Dutch Folk-Art Dish

The United States is like the whole world in one continent. People from all over the globe came to find a home in America. They brought their customs and way of life with them. Different groups of people settled in different parts of the country.

Today, most of the customs of the first settlers have disappeared. In one of the eastern states, however, life goes on just as it did a hundred years ago. The Amish people of the Pennsylvania Dutch country still dress and live as they did when they first arrived in America. These people are famous for their decorative art, which can be seen on the sides of barns, buildings, and in the crafts they make. You are going to make a dish with Pennsylvania Dutch designs on it. It will look lovely hanging on a wall in the kitchen.

Things You Need

white plastic plate
tracing paper
pencil
scissors
poster paints
watercolor paintbrush
kitchen cleanser
clear nail polish

Let's Begin

1. If you don't have a white plastic plate, paint a colored plate with white poster paint. Add kitchen cleanser to the paint if it does not stick to the plate.
2. Trace the heart, leaf, and feather shapes from the book onto a sheet of tracing paper. Notice that there are two sizes for each shape, one drawn inside the other. Trace the size which fits your plate best.
3. Cut out the heart, feather, and leaf shapes from the tracing page.
4. Using these as patterns, trace the heart on the top and bottom of the plate with a pencil, then on the left and right.
5. After the hearts are drawn, add a stem under each heart and a circle in the middle of the plate, Fig. a.
6. Trace two leaves next to each stem, Fig. b.
7. Trace the feather under each stem, Fig. b.
8. Add to the design by drawing a pair of eyes between each heart. An eye is drawn as a circle with a rainbow shape over it, Fig. c.
9. Paint the designs with bright colors.
10. To preserve your plate, brush over the painted designs with some of Mom's clear nail polish. Be sure that the paint has dried completely first.

Swiss-Cheese Candle

Before electricity was invented, candles were very important. They provided light for nighttime living. Pioneer people worked, ate, and read by candlelight. Today, candles are used mostly for decoration. You know that Mom puts them on your birthday cake, and there are probably other candles around the house which look pretty, but are not used for light. What you need is a fun candle you can make for yourself. Since you are going to make a Swiss-cheese candle, be sure that no one puts it in the refrigerator!

Things You Need

paraffin or canning wax
tall candle
play clay
milk carton
ice cubes
2 cooking pots, one larger than the other
hammer
dishcloth
butter
coffee cup
scissors

Let's Begin

1. Cut off the top of a milk container that has been washed and dried, Figs. a and b.
2. Grease the insides of the milk carton with the butter.
3. Put a piece of play clay on the bottom of the milk carton.
4. Push a candle about as tall as the carton straight into the play clay, Fig. c.
5. Place the cup in the large pot and fill the pot with water a little higher than the cup.
6. Put paraffin or canning wax into the smaller pot.
7. Place the pot which has wax in it on the cup, Fig. d.
**8. Put the bottom pot (containing the cup and smaller pot) on the stove burner. Turn on the flame, and allow the water to boil until the wax is melted. If the water begins to spill, lower the heat.
**9. When the wax has melted, empty a tray of ice cubes into a dishcloth or towel, Fig. e. Hammer the ice into smaller pieces. Do not overhammer.
10. Fill the milk container with the ice bits, Fig. f.
**11. Carefully pour the melted wax into the milk carton all the way to the top, Fig. g.
12. Let the candle harden for a half an hour. Put the carton in the sink, and peel it away, Fig. h. (There will be some water from the melted ice.) You have just unmolded your Swiss-cheese candle.

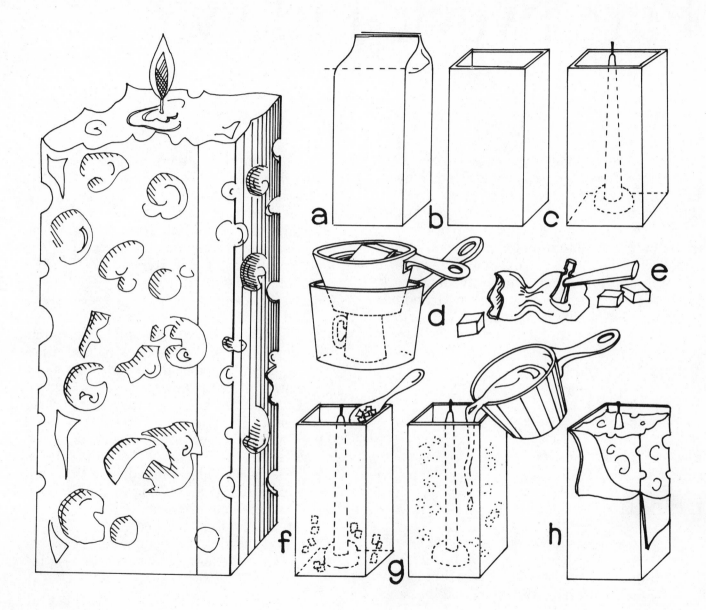

Patchwork Pillow

During the pioneer days, women saved all the scraps of material they could. Nothing was thrown away. Even the smallest piece of fabric could be used as a patch, or in a patchwork item. Patchwork objects are very pretty because of the combinations of different scraps which go into them. If you like to sew, then you will enjoy making this lovely patchwork pillow. It will make a lovely gift for Grandma. She might put it next to a patchwork quilt that her mother gave her.

Things You Need

scrap pieces of fabric
needle and thread
clothes iron
scissors
cotton stuffing

Let's Begin

1. Start by cutting about five equal length strips of different kinds of fabric. The fabrics can be of different thicknesses.
2. Place two strips together, making sure that their designs face one another, Fig. a.
3. Sew the two strips together, a little below the top edge, using the running stitch, Fig. b. (To do the stitch, see Ball-Fringe Apron, page 168.)
4. Sew the last stitch several times over itself before you cut the thread.
5. Sew all the other strips onto the first two, Fig. c.
**6. Use a medium-hot iron to flatten down all seams, Figs. d and e.
7. The front of the pillow will be the patchwork side. Make the back of the pillow by first placing the patchwork on a larger piece of fabric.
8. Cut out the back the same size as the front.
9. Place the front and the back together, Fig. f.
10. Sew the two pieces together with a running stitch near the edges, Fig. g.
11. Leave a little of one side unsewn.
12. Stuff the pillow with cotton stuffing.
13. Finish sewing the seam closed, Fig. h.
14. Go over the last stitch several times before you cut the thread.

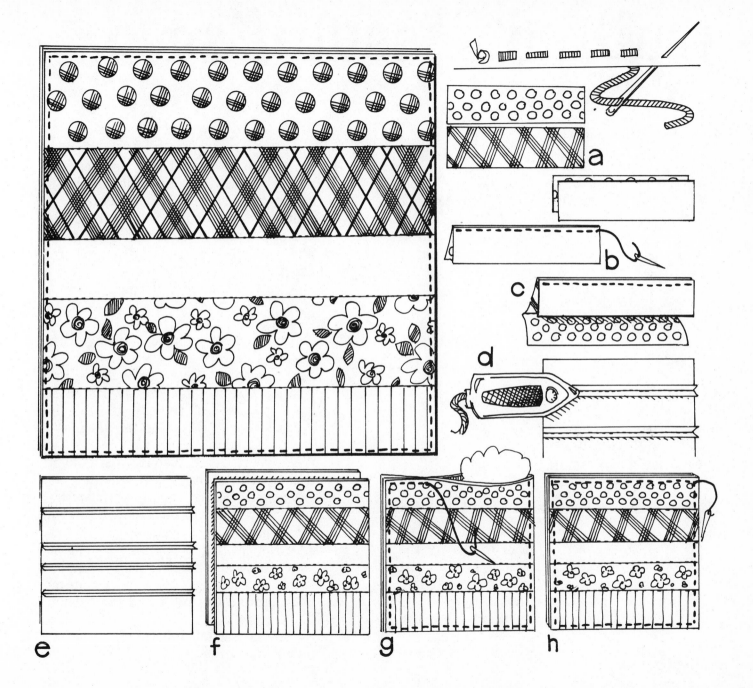

a

b

c

d

e f g h

Quilted Tissue Bag

Do you have a box of facial tissue in your home? It is time to throw it away—the box, that is. What you need is a tissue bag. The bag is so pretty because it is quilted. When you quilt, the designs appear to be raised against the background. This tissue bag is nice because you can hang it or lay it almost anywhere in your home.

Things You Need

safety pins
felt
cotton stuffing
scissors
needle with a large eye
1 sheet of tracing paper
pencil
embroidery thread

Let's Begin

1. Cut three pieces of felt of exactly the same size. Make them as big as you want the bag to be. A good size is indicated by the large bag in the illustration.
2. Trace the tulip and bow design from the book onto a sheet of tracing paper.
3. Pin this tracing onto one of the felt pieces with safety pins, Fig. a.
4. Spread some cotton stuffing in the center of another piece of felt.
5. Put the piece of felt with the pinned tracing on it over the piece of felt with the cotton stuffing. (The stuffing is sandwiched between the two felt pieces, Fig. b.)
**6. Thread a needle with a large eye using embroidery thread.
7. Sew a running stitch (to do it, see Ball-Fringe Apron, page 168) through the tracing as well as through the felt and cotton stuffing, following the outlines of the tulips, stems, and bow.
8. When you have finished sewing along all of the outlines, pull the tissue away.
9. Sew a small hem on the top of the quilted pieces of felt as well as the third piece of felt, Fig. c.
10. Hold the front and back of the bag together with all hems on the inside.
11. Sew the pieces together with a running stitch around the sides and the bottom, Fig. d.
12. Sew the last stitch several times before you cut the thread.

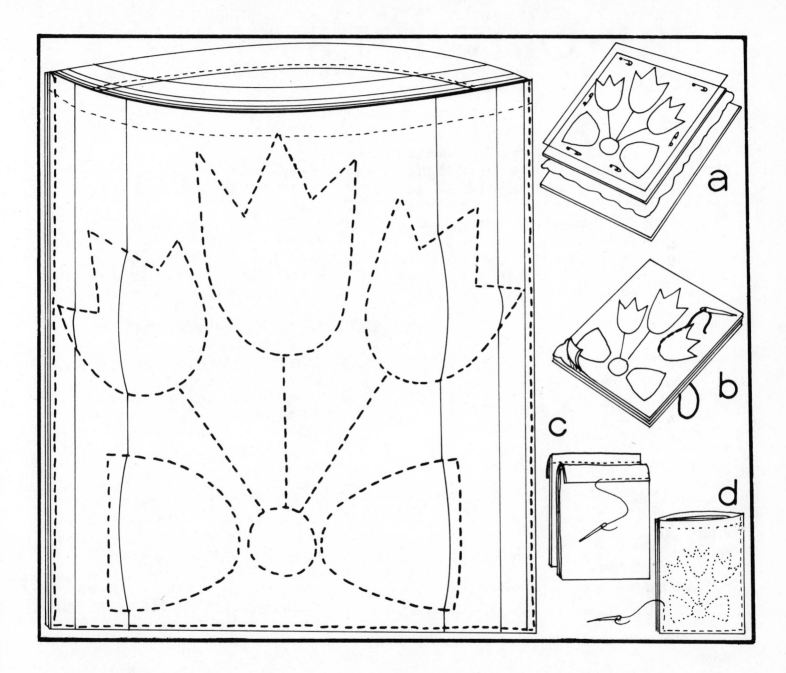

Play-Clay Pins

If you want to give a present to someone very special, a decorative pin is the ideal gift. These pretty pins will look wonderful on Grandma, and just as pretty on your Mom. Pin making is fun because it is like making cookies. You have to follow a recipe very carefully. Ask Mom for her help if you have a problem making the pins—she knows all about mixing and measuring.

Things You Need

2 cups cornstarch
4 cups baking soda
measuring cup
bowl
water
pot
poster paints
pencil
1 sheet of tracing paper
cardboard
rolling pin or soup can
spatula
wire rack or cookie sheet
pin backings (available at sewing counters)
liquid white glue
spoon and knife
watercolor brush
scissors
dishcloth
waxed paper

Let's Begin

1. Borrow some baking soda and cornstarch from Mom's kitchen.
2. Measure two cups of cornstarch and four cups of baking soda into a pot. Mix together with a spoon.
3. Add two and one-half cups of cold water to the mixture.
4. Place the pot over medium heat on the stove.
5. Stir everything together for about four minutes until the mixture has thickened to the consistency of mashed potatoes. Turn off the heat, and take the pot off the stove.
6. Cover the pot with a damp dishcloth.
7. When the dough has cooled, pick up half, and knead on a sheet of waxed paper for five minutes. That is, keep folding and pressing the dough with the thick part, or heel, of your hands.
8. Roll the dough between two sheets of waxed paper, not too thick or too thin (about one-quarter inch). Use a rolling pin or soup can.

(continued on page 194)

9. Trace the pin shapes (a–e) from the book onto a sheet of tracing paper. Cut out the shapes and trace them onto cardboard. Cut out the cardboard shapes.
10. Place the cardboard patterns on the dough and cut around the edges with a knife.
11. Remove the shapes with a spatula and place them on a wire rack or a cookie sheet.
12. Dry overnight. The thicker the cutouts, the longer they will take to dry.
13. Paint the designs on your pins with poster paints.
14. Glue a pin backing to the back of each pin with liquid white glue.

Playthings
from
other lands

Playthings from other lands

Have you ever traveled very far? Maybe you journeyed to the beach or to the mountains. Or was it a trip to Grandma's house? You must travel long distances to find out what games boys and girls in other countries play, and also what toys they play with. Some children buy toys at a department store. Many children have to make their own. If you have a good imagination, you can create a toy from a piece of paper or a piece of wood. Handmade toys are just as exciting as a toy made by a machine. It doesn't really matter how the toy was made. The important thing is how much fun it gives the kids who are playing with it.

What is your favorite toy? It might be a pretty doll, a toy soldier, or a rubber ball.

Children in different parts of Africa play kickball with a ball made from straw. It is shaped like a soccer ball. In Japan, children make dolls, buildings, and animals out of folded paper. All it takes is a piece of paper folded in the right place, and presto, a great toy is born.

If you think that all of these foreign toys sound exciting, just wait until you tackle some of the projects in this chapter. They are all easy to make. If one wears out or breaks, you can easily construct another instead of running to the store. Usually you have to wait until your next allowance to buy another toy. When you know the secrets of good, homemade fun, a new toy is just minutes away.

Mexican Piñata

The children in Mexico love special holidays. They get a chance to break a papier-mâché animal called a piñata. The children swing sticks at the piñata, which is filled with little toys and candy. When it is broken, everyone scrambles for the goodies. Piñatas come in all sizes and shapes. Your piñata is shaped like a big bird.

Things You Need
1 large brown paper bag
1 package of crepe paper
1 sheet of tracing paper
pencil
scissors
stapler or safety pins
tape or paper paste
cord
wrapped candies and small toys
baseball bat
colored construction paper

Let's Begin
1. Cut two packages of crepe paper into strips, Fig. a.
2. Cut a fringe along the bottom edge of each rolled strip, Fig. b. Open up the rolls. You will have long fringe strips.
3. Fill a large brown paper bag with candy and small toys.
4. Gather the bag at the opening, and staple or pin with safety pins, Fig. c. Bag should remain a little open.
5. Poke a hole into the top of both sides of the bag with a sharp pencil, Fig. c.
6. Pass a length of cord through each hole and tie, Fig. c.
7. Tie both cords together, Fig. d.
8. Hang the bag by this loop onto a door handle. You will now transform the bag into a funny bird.
9. To make the bird, tape or paste the fringed strips to the bag starting at the bottom. Keep taping on strips as you move up the bag. Let the fringed strips overlap a little bit.
10. Make the head of the bird a yellow paper circle with white-paper-circle eyes. Staple the head to the top of the bag.
11. The bird's beak shape is shown in the illustration. Trace the beak shape on a sheet of tracing paper.
12. Cut out the tracing and use it to trace a beak on orange construction paper.
13. Cut out the beak and fold it along the dotted lines.
14. Paste the beak to the head.
15. Cut out funny wings and feet from colored construction paper and tape or paste them to the fringed bag.
**16. Hang the piñata in a doorway or on a tree branch.
17. Each person is blindfolded and spun around. He then tries to break open the piñata with the bat.

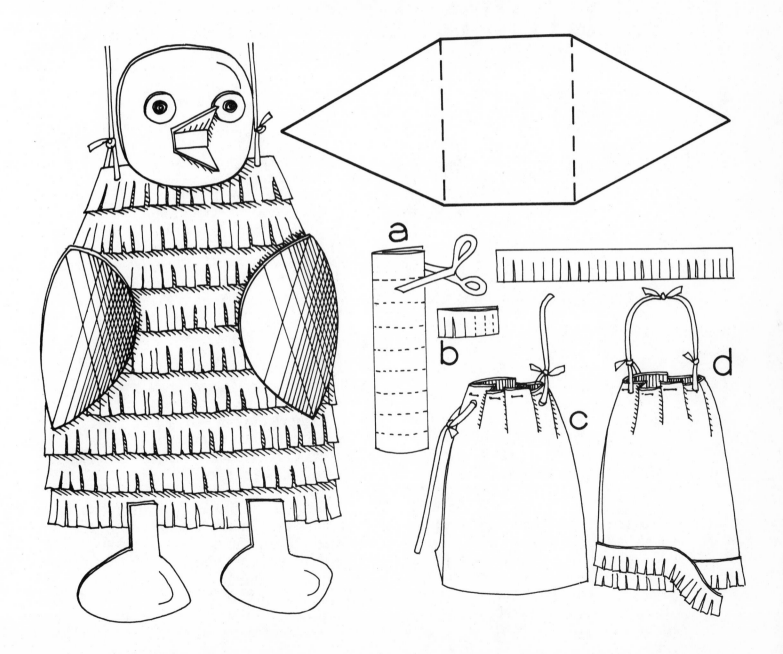

a

b

c

d

Ukrainian Pysanka Egg

It doesn't have to be Easter for you to enjoy dyeing eggs. The children of the Ukraine design some of the most spectacular dyed eggs. This craft looks very difficult but is well worth the effort it takes.

Things You Need

hard-boiled egg or blown egg (see below)
white crayon
egg or fabric dyes
small bowl

Let's Begin

**1. Use a hard-boiled egg or a blown egg. To blow out an egg, take a pin and twist it into the narrow end of an egg until it breaks through the shell, Fig. a.

**2. Remove the pin and make a hole in the other end. Make the hole on the wide end of the eggshell wider by chipping away a little bit of the shell with the pin.

3. Hold the egg over a small bowl and blow through the small hole in the narrow end of the shell. The insides of the egg will come out of the large hole in the egg.

4. Rinse the egg with cold water. Do not use soap.

5. The design is drawn on the egg with a white crayon. The design, as shown in the illustration, is drawn on both sides of the egg in the same way.

6. To copy the design, first draw two lines around the entire egg, from top to bottom and back to top, Fig. b.

7. Draw two lines going around the middle of the egg, Fig. c.

8. Draw a triangle in each "corner" of the egg on both sides, Fig. d.

9. Dip the egg in strong yellow dye solution.

10. Remove the egg and blot dry.

11. With the white crayon, fill in all the dark areas marked Number 1 in Fig. e.

12. Dip the egg in red dye solution.

13. Remove the egg and blot dry.

14. With the white crayon, fill in all the dark areas marked Number 2 in Fig. f.

15. Dip the egg in blue dye solution.

16. With white crayon, fill in all of the background, Number 3, in Fig. g.

**17. Hold the egg over the flame of a candle until the wax melts.

18. Wipe off the melted wax in a soft tissue.

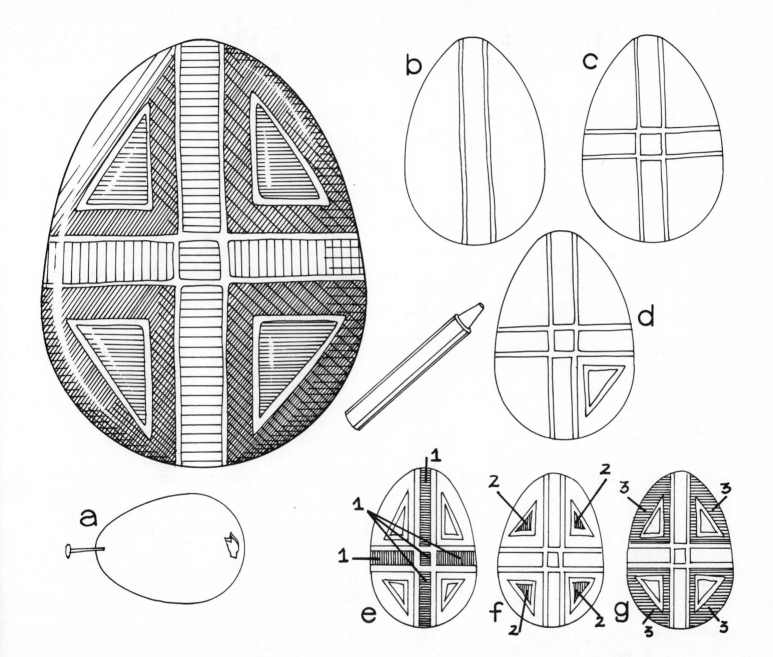

Japanese Origami Rocking Bird

The children of Japan enjoy making toys from paper. It is amazing what can be made from a simple sheet of paper. There is a name for this craft. It is called origami. The origami project shown on the opposite page is one of the most popular. The rocking bird can sit on your dresser or can be hung from the ceiling. If you make enough, you can have a flock of beautiful birds flying high above your room.

Things You Need

1 sheet of colored construction paper
crayons or colored felt-tipped markers
scissors
pencil

Let's Begin

1. Cut a piece of construction paper in a square (all sides equal).
2. Place the paper on the table so that the shape looks like a diamond, Fig. a.
3. Draw a small x and z in the corners that are on the left and right, Fig. a.
4. Fold corner x over to corner z making a sharp crease down the middle, Fig. b.
5. Bring corner x back to its original place, Fig. c.
6. Bring corner z to the fold in the center of the square and crease the corner down, Fig. d.
7. Bring corner x to the fold in the center of the square and crease the corner down, Fig. e.
8. Draw a small letter o on the new corners that are on the left and right.
9. Fold the paper in the middle so that both corners (letter o) meet, Fig. f.
10. Tilt the folded paper so corner o is on the bottom, Fig. g.
11. The tip of the paper shape (corner y in Fig. g) is then pushed down into the fold, Fig. h.
12. Use crayons or colored felt-tipped markers to draw eyes, wings, feathers, and feet on the bird.
13. Spread the bird apart slightly, and stand it on the two bottom points.
14. If you push on its tail, the bird will rock.

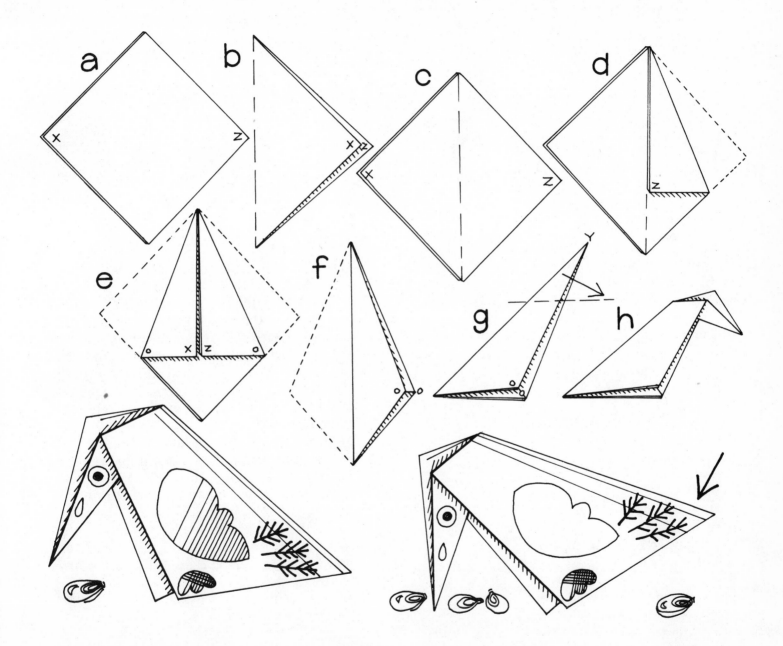

African Drum

The drum is one of the most interesting—and most primitive—of all musical instruments. In Africa it beats the rhythms of dances and songs, announces ceremonies and times of war.

The African drum you will make is modeled on an ancient instrument. It is a very pretty object and can be hung on a wall as well as "played."

Things You Need

oatmeal box
brown felt
yarn
poster paints
paintbrush
paper punch or a sharp pencil
scissors

Let's Begin

1. Paint an oatmeal box and its cover with a dark color.
2. Cut out two felt circles that are larger than the top of the box.
3. Punch an equal number of holes around the edge of the felt circles with a paper punch or with a sharp pencil, Fig. a.
4. Place a felt circle on the bottom and top of the box, Fig. b.
5. Tie one end of a long piece of yarn into one hole on the bottom circle of felt and knot it.
6. Bring the yarn up to a hole on the top felt circle, and push the yarn through.
7. Move the yarn down through another hole in the bottom circle and then up through a hole in the top circle.
8. Continue this process until you have gone completely around the box, filling all the holes of the felt circles with the yarn lacing.
9. If you need more yarn to finish the drum, tie an extra piece to the yarn already used.
10. Glue feathers to the top side of the drum.

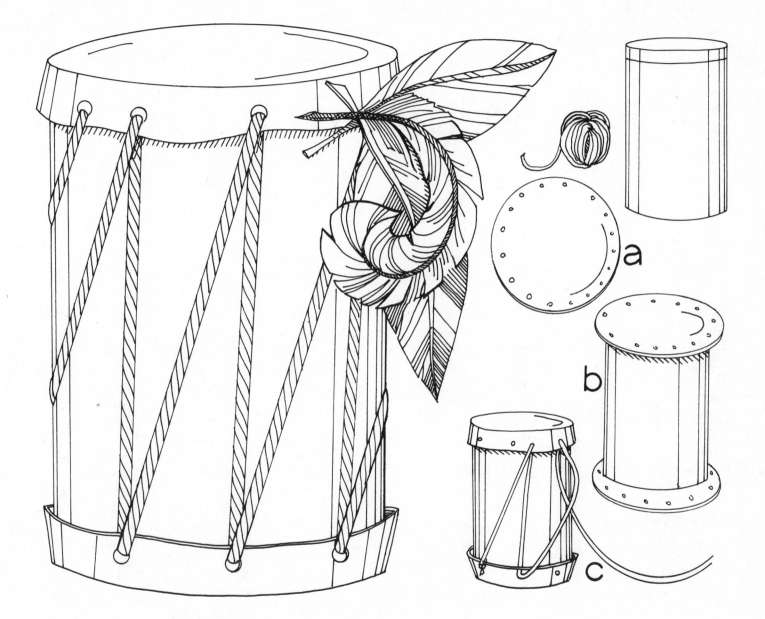

a

b

c

Polish Kaleidoscope Collage

Did you ever look into a kaleidoscope? A kaleidoscope is a small tube that contains small bits of colored glass and a reflecting mirror. When you look into the kaleidoscope and turn it, you see wonderful changing designs. Just as with snowflakes, you will never see two designs that look the same. If you like looking through a kaleidoscope, then you will enjoy this collage from Poland. It is just as beautiful and as colorful as any kaleidoscope design you will ever see.

Things You Need

colored construction paper
1 sheet of tracing paper
pencil
scissors
paper paste

Let's Begin

1. Trace all of the shapes from the book onto a sheet of tracing paper.
2. Cut out each shape. Trace two shapes each of d, e, f, g, and h, onto different-colored pieces of construction paper. Cut out shapes.
3. Trace remaining shapes onto a piece of construction paper that has first been folded. Place the dotted-line side of the shapes against the fold. Cut out two of each shape. When paper is opened, each shape is doubled to its complete form.
4. Draw a straight line across the center of a sheet of white construction paper.
5. Paste the flowers and leaves along the center line. Follow the drawing that shows where all the shapes should go.
6. Draw two stems going from the flowers to the center line.

Italian "Piggy in the Pen"

Here's a game that will test your skill. If you have lived on a farm you know how difficult it is to round up the pigs and get them in their pen. The pig in this toy is a ping-pong ball, and you have to get it into the box. Why not have a contest with your friends? See who will be the champion "Piggy in the Pen" player in your neighborhood. You'd better start practicing the minute you make it.

Things You Need

oatmeal box
cardboard tube from a roll of paper towels
scissors
length of yarn
ping-pong ball
liquid white glue
poster paints
paintbrush

Let's Begin

1. Trace around the end of the tube on the center bottom of an oatmeal box, Fig. a.
2. Poke a hole in the center of the drawn circle with a sharp pencil.
**3. Use this pencil hole to cut out the circle you drew on the bottom of the oatmeal box. Cut the circle a little smaller than the drawn circle.
4. Push one end of a paper-towel tube into the cutout circle.
5. For extra strength, spread glue around the place where the box and tube meet.
6. When the glue has dried, paint the box with poster paints and add designs if you wish.
**7. Twist a sharp pencil completely through the tube at a place a little below the bottom of the box, Fig. b.
**8. Twist a sharp pencil completely through a ping-pong ball, Fig. c.
9. Tie a length of cord or yarn through the holes in the tube and knot.
10. Tie the other end through the holes in the ping-pong ball and knot, Fig. d.
11. The idea of the game is to swing the ball up and try to catch it in the box. Hold the box by the tube and make an upward sweeping motion.

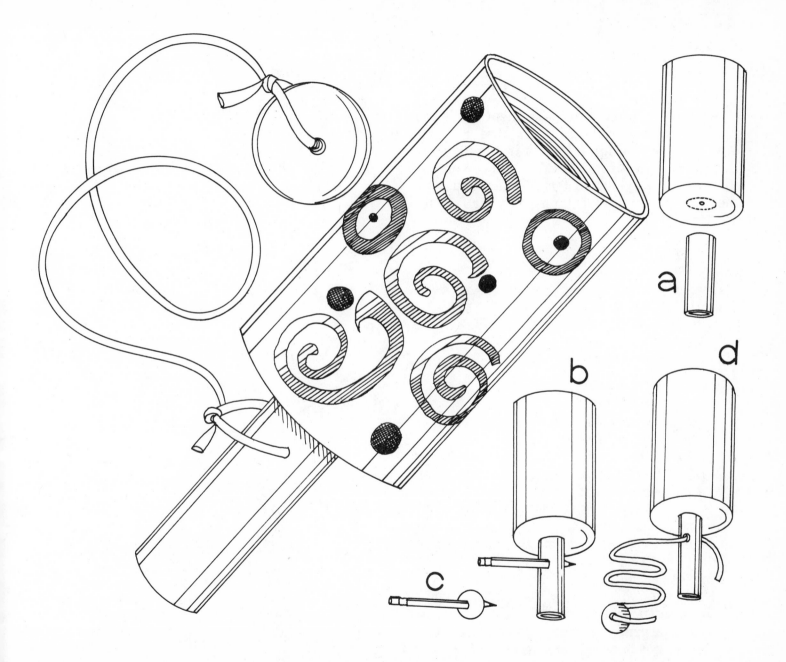

a

b

c

d

English Tops

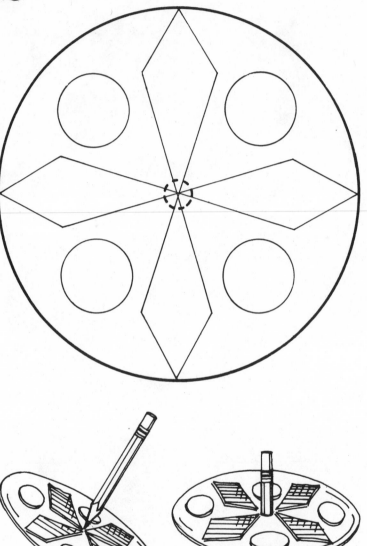

Tops are fun to play with. All they need is a twist of the fingers to make them go. Make yourself a large collection of these English tops. Only one design is shown in the illustration, but with your imagination you can create some really way-out patterns. When you spin the tops, they will make you and your friends dizzy.

Things You Need

1 sheet of tracing paper
1 short (used) pencil
crayons or colored felt-tipped markers
cardboard
colored construction paper

Let's Begin

1. Trace the circle shape from the book onto a sheet of tracing paper.
2. Cut out the tracing and use it to trace several circles on a piece of cardboard or construction paper.
3. Cut out the circles from the cardboard or construction paper.
4. Copy the design from the illustration, drawing it onto the circle with crayons or felt-tipped markers.
5. Push a small pencil with a sharp point through the center of the circle.
6. Spin the pencil, and let the top spin. See the designs it makes on paper.

Learning is what you like

Learning is what you like

Everybody around tells you that going to school is important, but sometimes it really seems dull. Other times, you find yourself liking school a lot. When it *is* fun, it's usually because you're talking or doing or thinking about things that really interest you. Whether it's dinosaurs or the planets or numbers or drawing—learning seems to be a matter of following your interest as far as it will take you.

Or discovering an interest you didn't know you had.

This chapter should help you make some of those discoveries. In it you will learn things you never knew about, or re-learn things you forgot you knew. The toys included in this chapter *are* educational, but, more important, they're fun. And fun just may be the best teacher you've ever had.

Playing the Alphabet

All languages have an alphabet. The alphabet is a picture list of sounds in the language. Some alphabets have more symbols, or pictures, than others. The Oriental people have pictures that represent whole words as well as sounds. The English language has twenty-six letters. It starts with the letter a, and ends with the letter z. Do you know the rest of the letters? It is one of the first things you learned. Now it is time to learn how to make new words.

Things You Need

crayons or colored felt-tipped markers
colored construction paper
scissors

Let's Begin

1. Cut twenty-six squares out of colored construction paper.
2. Draw a capital **A** on one side, and a small **a** on the other side of one of the squares.
3. Do the same with all of the letters in the alphabet on the remaining squares of construction paper.
4. Make words with the letters. Make words that cross on a common letter, like the words in a crossword puzzle. Invent word games using the letters as a deck of cards . . .

ABCDEFGHIJKLMNOPQRS TUVWXYZ

abcdefghijklmnopqrstuv wxyz

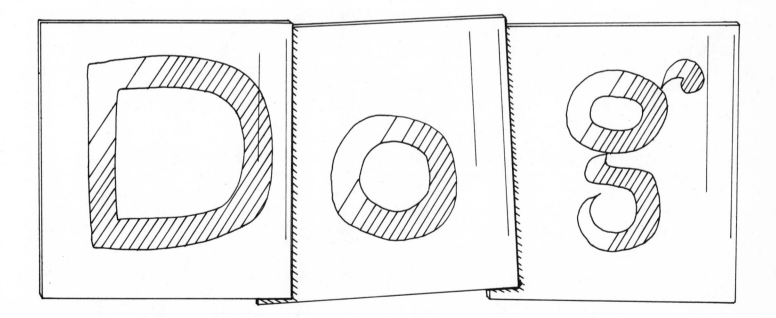

Learn to Count

"Countdown. 10, 9, 8, 7, 6, 5, 4, 3, 2, 1, blast-off!"

You hear these words whenever a rocket is being launched. This is a way of measuring time—of telling people how many seconds remain before the rocket leaves the ground. Numbers are symbols (pictures with a meaning) of quantities of things: 2 apples, 1 boy, 10 toys. Numbers are also written out: two apples, one boy, ten toys.

Numbers are useful because they tell us about how many things of anything there are. They are also used to help us determine the relations between quantities of things as in addition or subtraction. In other words, they are what we use to do mathematics.

Numbers are used everywhere. Everyone in the world knows and uses numbers. Now it's your turn to try . . .

Things You Need

paper

tracing paper
paper paste
pencil
scissors
crayons or colored felt-tipped markers

Let's Begin

1. Trace the circle with all its lines and numbers from the book onto a sheet of tracing paper.
2. Cut out the circle from the tracing paper.
3. Paste the tracing on a sheet of drawing paper.
4. Cut out the circle from the drawing paper.
5. Cut out the different numbers by cutting along the straight lines that cross through the circle, Fig. a.
6. Mix up the pie wedges, and try to put the circle back together as it was originally, Fig. b. The "secret" is to line up the short lines drawn along the edges of each wedge. If you match the short lines together, the numbers will go from 1 to 10.

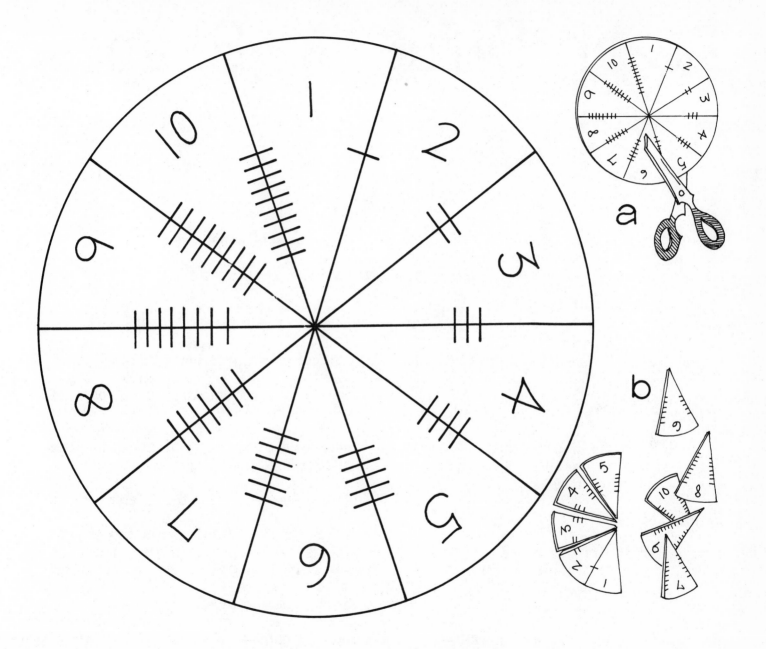

Learn Different Shapes

Probably one of the first toys your Mom gave you was a set of blocks. They were fun because you could stack one on top of another, and make all kinds of shapes. When you were finished playing with them, they could be knocked down and new shapes constructed. Every object has a shape. Certain shapes have special names. A wheel is a completely round shape—a circle. A block is square. If you put two blocks together, you will get a rectangle. Did you ever see a picture of a pyramid? It is shaped like a triangle. Now you can see how well you know the kinds of shapes. Start by looking in magazines and newspapers for circles, squares, and triangles.

Things You Need

1 large sheet of drawing paper
colored construction paper
1 sheet of tracing paper
pencil
scissors
crayons or colored felt-tipped markers
paper paste

old magazines or newspapers

Let's Begin

1. Trace the circle (Shape a), the triangle (Shape b), and the square (Shape c), onto a sheet of tracing paper.
2. Cut out the shapes from the tracing paper.
3. Use these shapes to trace a circle, triangle, and square, each onto construction paper of a different color.
4. Paste the shapes onto a large rectangular sheet of drawing paper, lining them along the left-hand side of the paper (see illustration).
5. Draw lines separating the different shapes as shown in the illustration.
6. Look through old magazines and cut out things that look like, or in part contain, the same shape as the shapes on the paper. (For example, an ice-cream cone has a triangle-shaped cone.)
7. Paste the shapes that match the circle, triangle, and the square next to the appropriate shape.

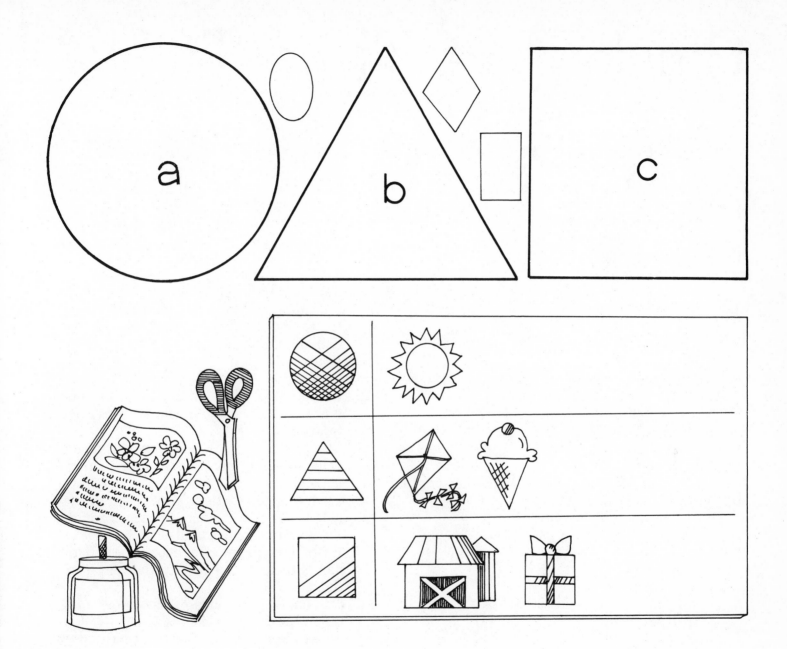

Clock-Face Time Teller

You hear the word "time" probably too many times during the day. "It's time to get up," says Mom. "It's time to correct your homework," says your teacher. "It's time to go to bed," says Dad. If you don't know how to tell time, it is *time* to learn. All you need is the Clock-Face Time Teller and a little instruction from Mom or Dad.

Things You Need

colored construction paper
piece of cardboard
1 sheet of tracing paper
crayons or colored felt-tipped markers
brass paper fastener
paper plate
pencil
scissors

Let's Begin

1. Trace around the edge of a large paper plate on a sheet of colored construction paper.
2. Cut out the circle.
3. Paste the circle on a sheet of cardboard. Cut out the circle from the cardboard.
4. Punch a hole in the center of the cardboard with a sharp pencil.
5. To place the numbers on the clock, first draw the 12 on the top and the 6 on the bottom of the circle.
6. Draw the 3 on the right and the 9 on the left of the circle, Fig. a.
7. Draw the other numbers between the numbers you have already drawn on the circle.
8. Trace the hands of the clock from the book onto a sheet of tracing paper. Draw the entire arrow for the big hand. Draw the arrow up to the dotted line for the little hand.
9. Draw a small hole on each hand where indicated.
10. Cut out the tracings and use them to trace the arrows onto colored construction paper.
11. Cut out the hands and punch a small hole on the bottom of each with a sharp pencil.
12. Push a paper fastener first through the hole in the little hand and then through the hole in the big hand, Fig. b.
13. Push the paper fastener with both hands through the hole in the center of the clock.
14. Spread the two ends of the paper fastener apart on the back of the clock.
15. Move the hands to tell time just like a real clock.

a

b

Learn about Money

Now you can have all the play money you always wanted. The purpose of this money is to help you understand the units of money. The dollar is the basic unit. You probably don't see too many of them in your pocket. But you do see a lot of coins. Pennies, nickels, dimes, and quarters are nice to have. You can buy bars of candy or toys with them. Do you know how many pennies in a nickel or in a dollar? If you are curious, get started on this project right away.

Things You Need

colored construction paper
1 sheet of tracing paper
pencil
scissors
crayons or colored felt-tipped markers

Let's Begin

1. Trace all of the circles from the book onto a sheet of tracing paper.
2. Cut out the circles from the tracing paper and use them to trace lots of different circles on colored construction paper. That is, many of each size.
3. Cut out the traced circles.
4. There are 100 pennies in a dollar.
   The large circle, Shape a, is a half-dollar. It represents 50 pennies.
   Shape b is a quarter. It represents 25 pennies.
   Shape c is a nickel. It represents 5 pennies.
   Shape d is a penny. There are—how many pennies in a dollar?
   Shape e is a dime. Even though it is smaller than a penny, it represents 10 pennies.
5. Mix and match the circles until you have one dollar. Here is one example: one dollar equals one half-dollar (50¢), plus one quarter (25¢), plus one dime (10¢), plus two nickels (5¢ each), plus five pennies (1¢ each).

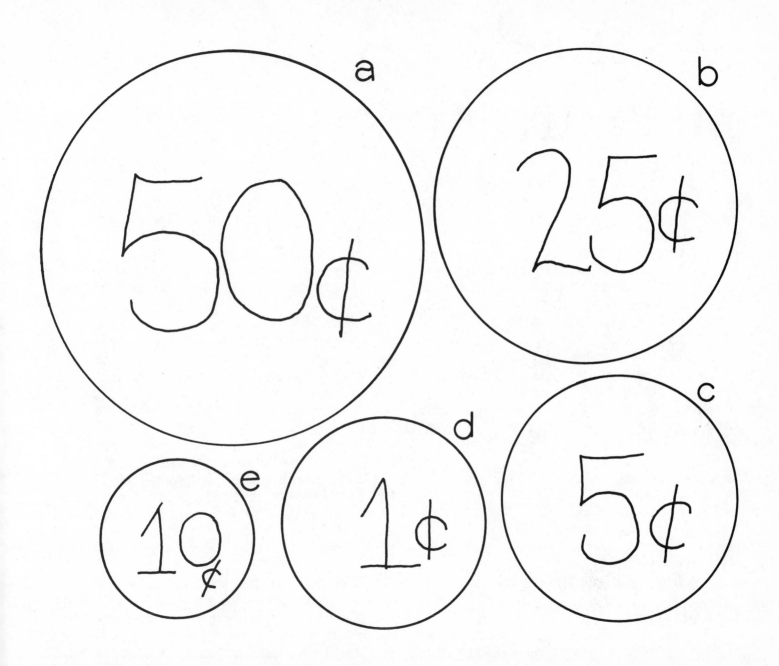

Centipede Measure-Maker

Do you know what an inch, a foot, and a yard are? They are measurements of length. Something can be an inch long, a foot long, or a yard long. When Mom measures you to see how tall you are, she uses feet and inches. When she wants to see how much you have grown from one year to another, she uses inches. You can grow one or two inches in a year. When she buys fabric, she buys it by the yard. These words are very important, and you should know something about them.

The centipede you will make will help you remember how many inches are in a foot, and how many feet are in a yard. It even shows you how long an inch is. Mom might even want to use it when she is making a new dress.

Things You Need

colored construction paper
1 sheet of tracing paper
pencil
scissors
crayons or colored felt-tipped markers

Let's Begin

1. Trace the three circle shapes, a, b, and c, onto a sheet of tracing paper.
2. Cut out the traced circles and trace them onto colored construction paper.
3. Trace one Shape a on red construction paper, and draw a silly face on it.
4. Trace thirty-two Shape b circles on red construction paper. Draw a line down the middle of each circle with a crayon or colored felt-tipped marker.
5. Trace three Shape c circles on blue construction paper. Draw a star on each circle (see illustration).
6. Cut out all circles.
7. The centipede will be a yard long. A yard is made up of thirty-six inches, which is the number of circles you cut out including the head. A yard can also be broken down into three feet. Each foot is twelve inches long. To make your centipede, first put down his head, the red circle, which represents the first inch.
8. To make a foot, add eleven more inches or circles.
9. Each foot ends on the twelfth inch. Mark the twelfth inch with a blue circle. When all of the circles are in place you will have a centipede that is one yard, or three feet, or thirty-six inches long.

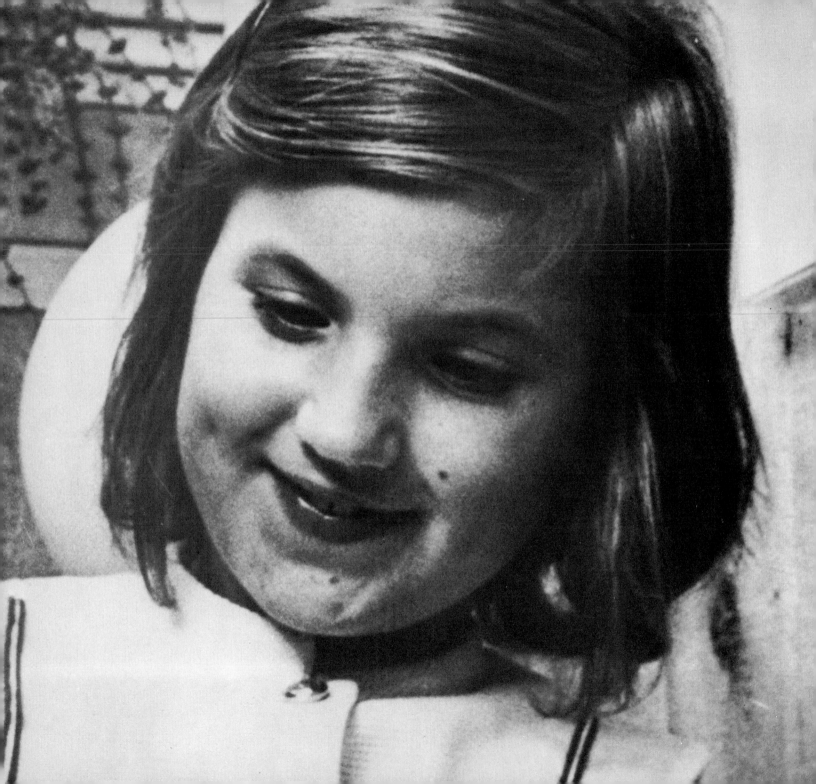

Tasty tummy ticklers

Tasty tummy ticklers

Eating is fun, but have you ever tried to cook? Watching Mom or Dad in the kitchen putting together something delicious is a fascinating experience indeed. Take a home-made cake. First there's the slippery beautiful eggs, which you've no doubt learned how to break yourself. Then a little sugar, some good butter, flour, flavoring, stirring. (People use electric mixers nowadays, but really, you should stir a batter at least once in a while by hand. You feel what it's like to put a cake together with muscle.) Now the careful baking until the layers have risen high and are tender and golden. What about chocolate icing? What about it! Is there anything better than scraping the icing bowl with your finger and popping a delicious lick of chocolate in your mouth? The finished cake is a sweet beauty. You wonder at the pleasure of making something and then being able to eat it. It seems almost too good to be true.

Now you can get into that mixing bowl with more than a finger's worth. You will be making many things to eat that will not only taste good but be unusual-looking (like the Happy Ice-Cream Clown). If you have helped Mom in the kitchen, now is her time to help you. Together you will create tasty tummy ticklers for you and your whole family to enjoy.

Happy Ice-Cream Clown

You've seen the clowns at the circus with their baggy pants and funny faces. But have you ever seen one made of ice cream? Now's your chance to make a refreshing ice-cream clown that you and your friends will love. You'll have a circus of fun in your own house making and eating this delicious snack.

Things You Need

ice cream, any flavor you like
ice-cream scoop
ice-cream cones
regular and miniature marshmallows
small candies for the eyes
gel icing in a tube
paper dishes
spoons

Let's Begin

1. Make the clown's hat from an ice-cream cone to which you've attached three small marshmallows with a dab of gel icing from a tube.
2. Place a scoop of ice cream on a paper plate, Fig. a.
3. Make the clown's collar from a row of marshmallows arranged around the bottom of the scoop, Fig. b.
4. Make the face using small round candies for the eyes, a miniature marshmallow for the nose, and gel icing from a tube for the smile, Fig. c.
5. Put the cone hat on the clown's head and eat with a spoon. Or put the clown in the freezer and enjoy later on.

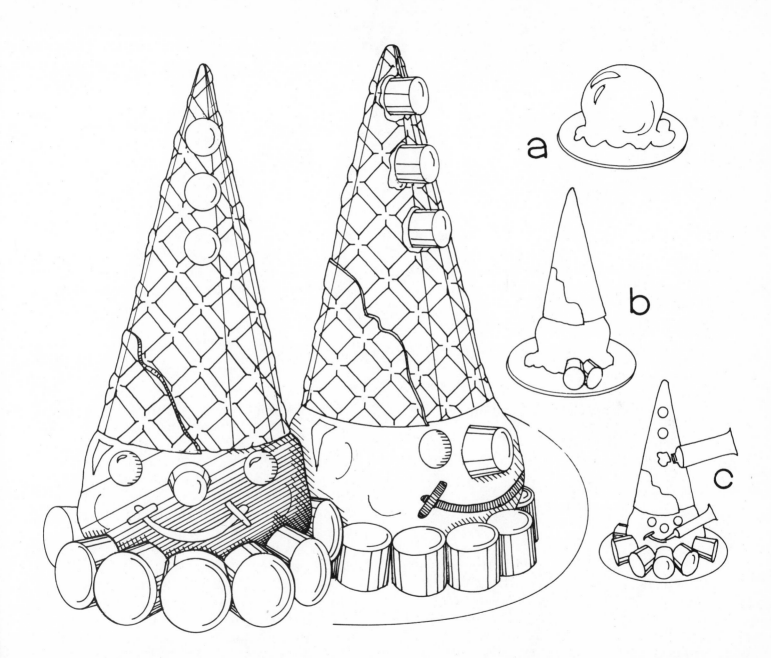

a

b

c

Marshmallow Boy and Dog

Owning a dog is a lot of fun. It is like having another brother or sister. Dogs love being with you and you love being with them. Now you can "create" the love of a boy and his dog in your kitchen. Or, at least, you can make a delicious marshmallow treat in the shape of the two companions.

Things You Need

regular and miniature marshmallows
toothpicks
colored construction paper
gel icing in a tube ·
tape

Let's Begin

THE BOY
1. Make the boy's body from three regular marshmallows put together with toothpicks.
2. Make an arm from two miniature marshmallows on a toothpick. Make two arms and push them into the middle of the body.
3. Make a leg from three miniature marshmallows on a toothpick. Make two legs and push them into the underside of the bottom marshmallow.
4. Make the cone hat by rolling a paper half-circle into a cone shape and taping it; put it on top of the head.
5. Draw a face on the boy with gel icing from a tube.

THE DOG
1. Make the dog's body from two regular marshmallows put together with toothpicks.
2. Make the head from another regular marshmallow put on the body with toothpicks. The head should be attached a little higher than the body.
3. Make a leg from two miniature marshmallows on a toothpick. Make four legs and push them into the body, two to the underside of each marshmallow.
4. Make the nose, tail, and two ears from miniature marshmallows by attaching them to the face with toothpick halves.
5. Draw on gel-icing eyes.

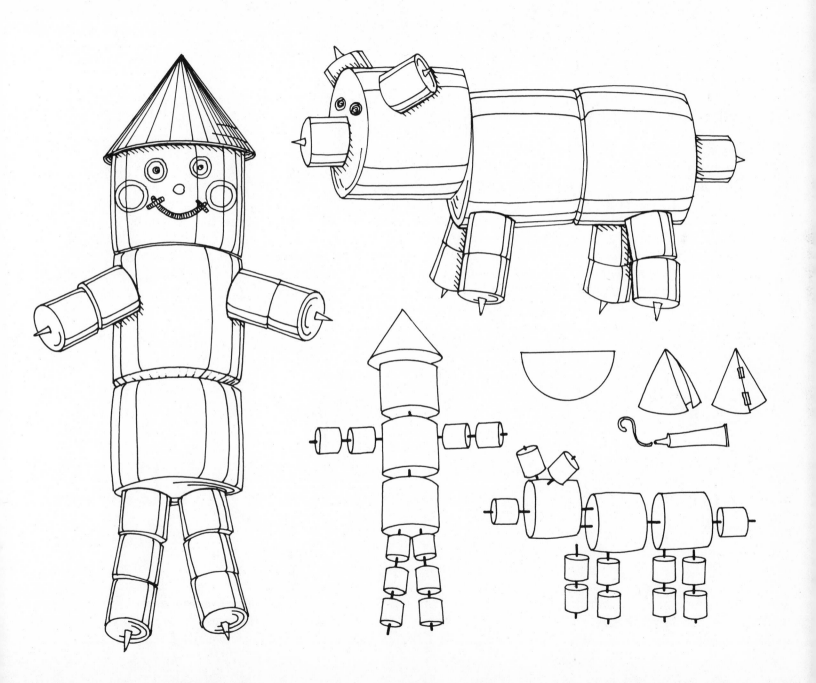

Decorate a Cupcake

Cupcakes are little cakes that can be eaten all by yourself. If you have a big appetite, a cupcake can be in your tummy in a few minutes. A large cake has to be cut into slices and shared by everyone because it is too big to be gobbled up by one person. Not the cupcake, which is like your own private treat. (Although it is always best to make baked goods from scratch, we will use mixes here to get you started fast.)

Things You Need

box of cupcake mix
cupcake pans
flutted paper muffin or cupcake cups
regular and miniature marshmallows, cookies
and candies (see below for specific kinds)
frosting or gel icing in a tube
box of white frosting mix
box of chocolate frosting mix
food coloring

Let's Begin

1. Following the instructions on the box of cupcake mix, make the cupcake batter.
2. Place a paper muffin cup into each cupcake shape in your cupcake pan.
3. Spoon the batter into the cups filling them half full, Fig. a.

**4. Bake following package directions.
5. Decorate the cooled cupcakes following the ideas below, Fig. b.

HAPPY FACES
1. Frost a cupcake with pink, yellow, or chocolate frosting. Tint white frosting with food coloring to get pink or yellow.
2. Make the eyes from small round candy, the nose from a miniature marshmallow, the cheeks from large flat candies, and the mouth from a licorice string.

NAME CUPCAKES
1. Frost a cupcake with chocolate frosting.
2. Draw on a name with white icing from a tube.

SPRING DAISY
1. Frost a cupcake with white or colored frosting.
2. Make the petals from large flat round candies and the core from a small round candy.
3. Add a spearmint leaf and a licorice-string stem.

FUNNY ANIMALS
1. Frost a cupcake in any funny color.
2. Make animal ears from two cookies.
3. Make the nose from a large marshmallow or gumdrop, the eyes from round candy, and the mouth from tube frosting.

Funny-Shape Cake Bake

Now is the time for all good (or only so-so good) kids to bake a cake. Or many cakes—the recipe below allows you to assemble and decorate your layers in a variety of interesting, funny ways. Although you will use a mix, you should be very, very proud of the results. Why, some of the cakes will look so good, you may not want to cut into them!

Things You Need

box of cake mix, your favorite flavor
2 round or square baking pans
knife
packaged frosting mix
frosting or gel icing in a tube
candies (licorice stick for Sail Boat and
   marshmallow for Mr. Rabbit)
food coloring

Let's Begin

**1. Following the instructions on the box, make the cake batter.
**2. Bake the cake mix in either two square or two round baking pans.
3. Assemble and decorate your cake when it has cooled following any of the ideas below.

THE BASEBALL
1. Put two round layers together with white frosting between them, then frost the entire cake.
2. Draw stitch designs on the cake with blue icing from a tube.

THE WRAPPED BOX
1. Put two square layers together with chocolate frosting between them, then frost the entire cake.
2. Draw a ribbon with red frosting from a tube and make a name tag with white frosting.

SMILING SUN
**1. Cut out wedges along the outer edge of one round cake layer with a knife, Fig. a.
2. Place the second round layer on a large platter.
3. Stick all of the wedges you cut from the first layer onto the outer edge of the second layer with a dab of frosting.
4. Frost the top of this layer with orange frosting, Fig. b.
5. Put the first layer (the one with the wedges cut out) on top of the layer on the plate.
6. Frost the top of this layer with yellow frosting.

(continued on page 238)

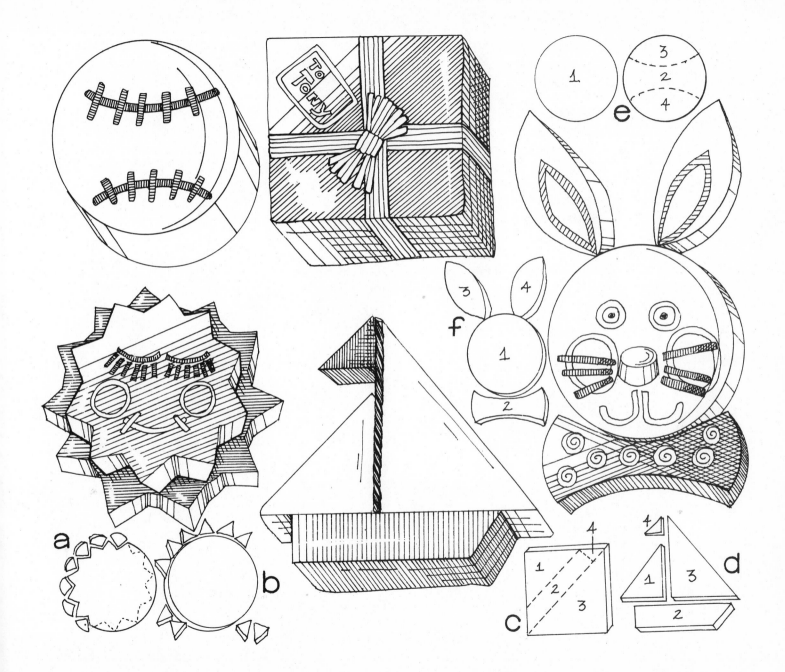

e

1
3
2
4

f
3
4
1
2

a

b

c
4
1
2
3

d
4
1
3
2

To
Tony

7. Decorate the cake with tube frosting.

SAIL BOAT
1. Put two square layers together with white frosting between them.
**2. Cut the stacked layers as shown in Fig. c.
3. Arrange the cake pieces to form a boat as shown in Fig. d. Leave space between pieces.
4. Frost the sails white, the boat and flag red (tint white frosting with red food coloring).
5. Put a licorice-stick mast between the sails and touching the flag. Push pieces together.

MR. RABBIT
**1. Cut one round layer as shown in Fig. e.
2. Arrange these pieces around the second uncut layer as shown in Fig. f.
3. Frost the face and ears with white frosting.
4. Frost the bow tie with yellow frosting (tint white frosting with yellow food coloring).
5. Use tube frosting to draw the face, and a marshmallow for the nose.

Fairy-Tale Castle

It would be wonderful to see some of the fabulous things you read about in fairy tales. Things like castles with their moats and turrets and towers, their battlements and flags and damsels in distress. Do you like castles? If you do, why not make your own? It will look—and be—good enough to eat.

Things You Need

shoe box
oatmeal or salt box
aluminum foil
ice-cream cones
assorted cookies
candies
marshmallows
frosting in a tube
colored construction paper
liquid white glue
toothpicks

Let's Begin

1. Cover a shoe box and the oatmeal or salt box with aluminum foil, Fig. a.
2. Glue the round oatmeal or salt box to the end of the shoe box, Fig. b.
3. Let the glue dry.
4. Stick the cookies to the foil-covered boxes with a little dab of frosting from a tube, Fig. c.
5. Add candies and marshmallows the same way you did with the cookies.
6. Top the castle with different-shaped ice-cream cones.
7. Make flags from triangles of colored construction paper and glue them to toothpicks.
8. Push the toothpicks into the tops of the ice-cream cones.
9. Add any other eatable decorations you please—use your imagination!

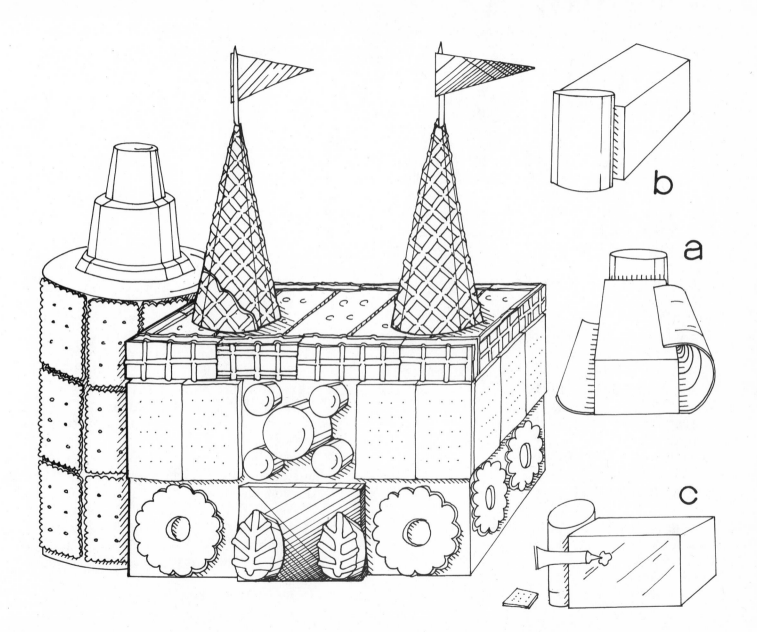

b

a

c

Everyone Loves Sugar Cookies

There are so many cookies for sale that it is difficult to have just one favorite. You probably like Mom's cookies the best. If you like homemade cookies, then you should make a batch of your own. Your cookies will be so delicious it is going to be difficult keeping Mom and Dad out of your cookie jar.

Food Things You Need

4 cups sifted flour
2½ teaspoons baking powder
½ teaspoon salt
⅔ cup soft butter
1½ cups granulated sugar
2 eggs
1 teaspoon vanilla extract
4 teaspoons milk
gel icing or frosting in a tube

Baking Things You Need

2 large bowls
waxed paper
cookie sheet
cookie rack
rolling pin
spatula

Other Things You Need

tracing paper
pencil
cardboard
paper
scissors

Let's Begin

1. Mix the flour, baking powder, and salt in a large bowl.
**2. Cream the butter and sugar together in another large bowl until the mixture is light and fluffy. Beat in the eggs and blend well. Add the milk and vanilla extract. Stir the mixture until it seems nice and light.
3. Slowly add the dry ingredients to the butter mixture, stirring everything until well blended.
4. Place the dough in the refrigerator.
5. Make cookie patterns by tracing the gingerbread boy, bird, and fish shapes from the book onto a sheet of tracing paper.
6. Trace the girl and boy cookie shapes. Follow the dotted lines for the girl shape.

242

(continued on page 244)

7. Cut out the tracings and, using them as patterns, trace shapes onto a sheet of cardboard.

8. Cut out the cardboard shapes.

**9. When the dough is firm enough to handle, turn on the oven to 400 degrees.

10. Sprinkle a sheet of waxed paper with a little flour. Put part of the dough on the paper. Keep the rest of the dough in the refrigerator.

11. Flatten the dough and put another piece of waxed paper over it. Roll the dough between the two sheets of waxed paper with a rolling pin, Fig. a.

12. Place a cardboard cookie pattern on top of the dough.

13. Cut the dough around the cookie shape, Fig. b.

14. Lift the cookie with a spatula, and put it on a buttered cookie sheet, Fig. c.

**15. Using whichever patterns you want, cut out cookies. Place several on a cookie sheet, and bake for ten minutes, or until they look brown.

**16. Remove the cookie with a spatula, and let them cool on a plate or a cookie rack.

17. Decorate the cold cookies with gel icings or frostings from a tube, Fig. d.

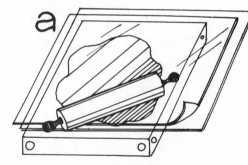

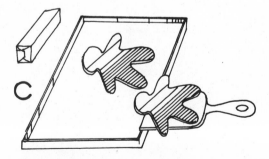

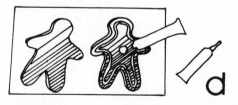

Let's have
a party

Let's have a party

Every year has many special days which are set aside for honoring people and events. There are the big holidays that everyone celebrates—things like Christmas and New Year's—and the special occasions observed and enjoyed by your friends and family only. Whatever the occasion, why not have a party (with Mom's permission, of course)? Whether its your birthday or George Washington's, it's great to get together with people you like to have fun.

Of course, you can go to the store to get "fancy" party fixings—or you can make them yourself. Read on and learn how to make all your own party decorations and favors—things like hats, noisemakers, and confetti balloons—as well as exciting games to play (have some small prizes or pennies on hand for the winners). This chapter will show you how to create your own invitations—in fact, how to get all the fun together and going. Take out your calendar and circle the day you want your party to happen. Then start to make things. And by all means—have a good time!

Special Invitations

If you're going to give a party you will want to invite all of your friends. How are you going to let them know what day and what time the party will be? Send a handmade invitation. This special invitation has three messages inside it. The outside announces your party. When your friends open it, the date and the time come into view. One look at your invitation and everyone will wish your party were tomorrow.

Things You Need

colored construction paper
1 sheet of tracing paper
pencil
scissors
crayons or colored felt-tipped markers

Let's Begin

1. Trace the cake shape from the book onto a sheet of tracing paper.
2. Cut a long strip of colored construction paper as high as the traced cake.
3. Cut out the tracing and use it to draw a cake on one side of the strip of paper, Fig. a.
4. Fold the paper on the left dotted edge of the cake drawing, Fig. b.
5. Fold the paper back along itself from the right dotted edge, Fig. c. Trim any excess paper away.
6. Cut around the cake except at the sides where there is a dotted line, Fig. d.
7. Use crayons or colored felt-tipped markers to decorate the front of the invitation as if it were a fancy cake.
8. Inside the card, write the place of the party, the day, and the time it will begin and end.

Surprise Favors

Parties—and especially birthday parties—frequently bring presents to you, the party-giver or guest of honor. A nice way to return the compliment is to provide favors for your guests. These Surprise Favors contain candy and may also be used as place cards at the table.

Things You Need

cardboard tubes from bathroom-tissue rolls
colored tissue paper
tape
scissors
wrapped hard candy
ribbon
colored construction paper
paper punch
crayons or colored felt-tipped markers

Let's Begin

1. Collect cardboard tubes from bathroom-tissue rolls long before the day of your party.

2. Fill each tube with wrapped candy.
3. Place the filled roll on a large sheet of colored tissue paper (also try colored cellophane or gift wrap), Fig. a.
4. Roll the paper around the tube and tape it together, Fig. b.
5. Tie the excess tissue onto one end of the favor with a length of ribbon or yarn. Keep one end of the ribbon long.
6. Cut a small name tag from colored construction paper.
7. Write the name of the person on the tag with crayons or colored felt-tipped markers.
8. Punch a hole on one end of the name tag.
9. Tie the long end of the ribbon into the punched hole in the tag, Fig. c.
10. Tie the other end of the favor with a shorter piece of ribbon.
11. Cut slits into the side paper frills to make a feathery fringe, Fig. d.

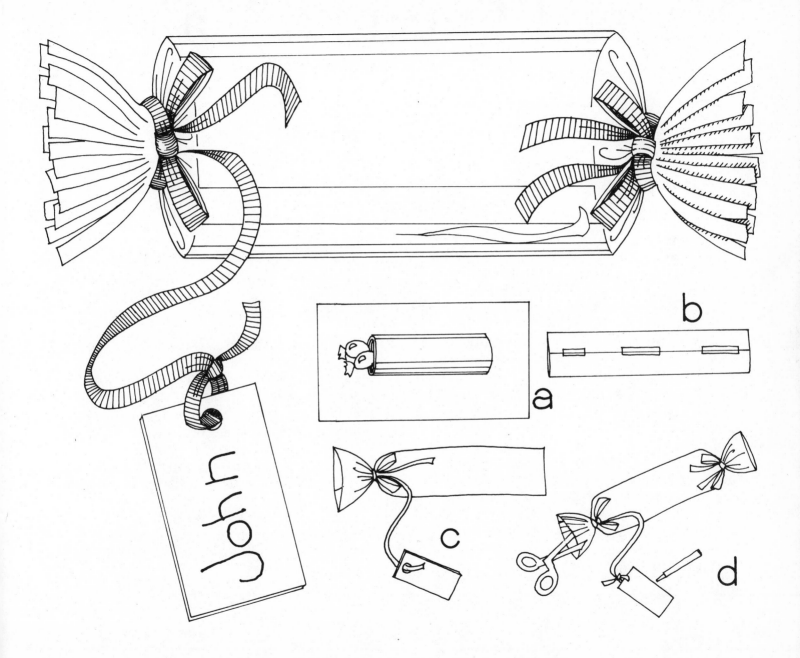

John

a

b

c

d

Paper Captain's Hat

Your party won't be complete unless your guests have hats to wear on their heads. You can go to the store and buy the pointed paper hats, but why not be different this year? Since you are going to make everything for your party, you should make the hats as well. All you need is a package of construction paper and you will be in business. Make the hats in all colors. Don't worry about the sizes. The bigger they are, the more fun your guests will have with them on their heads. If you really want to show your friends how creative you are, decorate your captain's hats with feathers or marshmallows, or draw designs on them.

Things You Need

large sheets of colored construction paper or
   large sheets of drawing paper
stapler

Let's Begin

1. Fold a large sheet of paper in half along the short side or width, Fig. a.
2. Keep the folded part on top and draw a line down the center of the paper, Fig. a.
3. Fold the two top corners, marked in the illustration with a letter x, over to the middle line on the paper, Figs. b and c.
4. Fold one of the bottom ends of the paper, marked with a letter z, over the two folded corners, Fig. d.
5. Turn the paper over, and do the same with the other bottom end, Figs. e and f.
6. Staple both ends of the hat (see illustration).
7. Decorate the hats with paper feathers or designs drawn with crayon or colored felt-tipped markers.

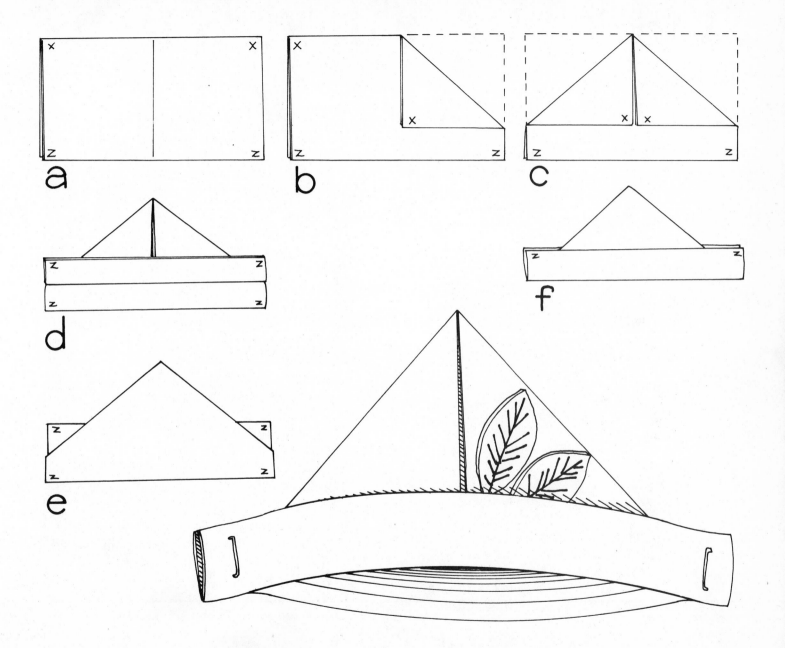

a

b

c

d

e

f

Four Fun-Filled Games

One of the fun parts of any party is playing games. Some of your favorite party games are pin the tail on the donkey and bobbing for apples. Now you will have four more fun-filled games to play. (With so much to do, you may not have any time to eat your cake and goodies.)

Things You Need

colored construction paper (including 1 large sheet)
tape
paper paste
crayons or colored felt-tipped markers
paper cups
rubber ball
soup cans
marshmallows
thread
string
drinking glass

Let's Begin

PIN THE NOSE ON THE CLOWN
1. Make the clown face from a large circle of light-colored construction paper. Make his hat from a triangle of blue paper. His collar can be any shape and any color.
2. Paste the face, hat, and collar onto a large sheet of white paper (see illustration).
3. Draw hair and eyes.
4. Make several noses by tracing around the edge of a drinking glass on red construction paper. Cut out the circles.
5. Hang the clown face on the wall.
6. Blindfold each guest and give him a nose that has a piece of tape attached to it.
7. Spin the person around, and see if he can pin the nose in the middle of the clown's face.

PAPER-CUP BOWLING
1. Place ten cups on the floor as shown by the triangle of circles in the illustration.
2. The aim of the game is to roll a rubber ball and try to knock down all of the cups.
3. Add up the scores. The person with the most points in five rolls wins a prize.

PENNY TOSS
**1. Remove the labels from tin cans by soaking them in warm water.
2. Write the numbers 1 to 5 on each can with an indelible felt-tipped marker.
3. Put the cans together on the floor.
4. Guests toss pennies onto the cans. If one lands in the can you win the number of pennies written on the can.

KISSING MARSHMALLOWS
**1. Thread a marshmallow onto a long length of cotton thread.
2. Hang it from a doorway.
3. A girl and a boy try to bite the hanging marshmallow at the same time.

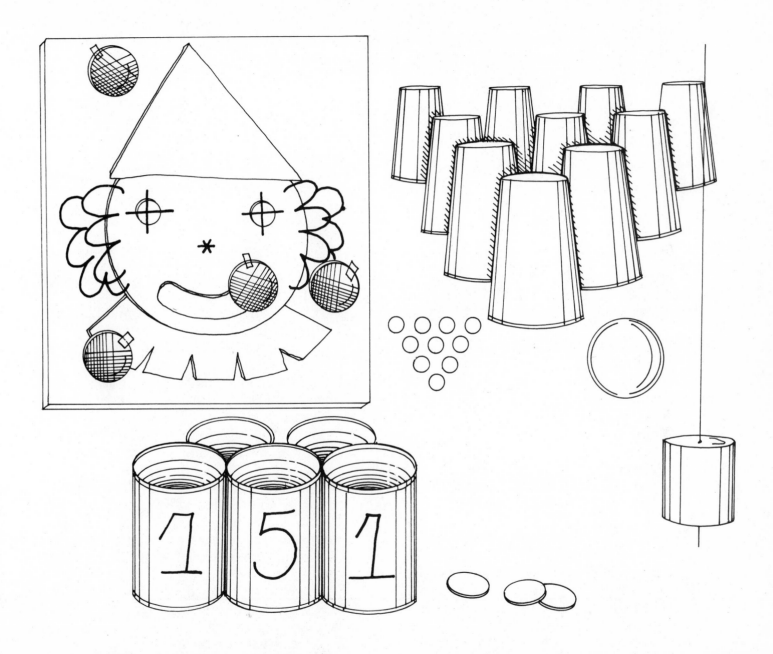

Snapping Pop Guns

Noisemakers, horns, and rattlers are old friends at parties. To the familiar kinds you will want to add these Snapping Pop Guns. They are very easy to make. All you need is a stack of typewriter paper and a pencil. Make a boxful of these paper guns. You might want to use them after a party when you play with your friends.

Things You Need

1 sheet of typewriter paper or 1 sheet of newspaper
pencil

Let's Begin

1. The larger the paper the louder the pop. The paper should be longer than it is wide. Fold the paper in half along the long side.
2. Open the paper again.
3. Draw a small letter x on all four corners.
4. Fold all corners to the folded line marked with a letter z, Fig. a.
5. When all corners are in the middle, fold the paper in half, Fig. b. Folded corners should be inside. The folded line marked with the letter z is now on top.
6. Fold the paper in half again so that both corners marked with the letter z are together, Fig. c.
7. Fold the top edge of the corner z which faces you down so that it lies against the paper, Fig. d.
8. Turn the paper around and do the same with the other corner z, Fig. e.
9. To make the gun pop, first hold the two points marked letter z in your hand with the folded inside part facing away from you.
10. Snap your wrist hard. The folded inside part will pop out making a noise.
11. To pop the gun again, push the folded inside part back into the gun.

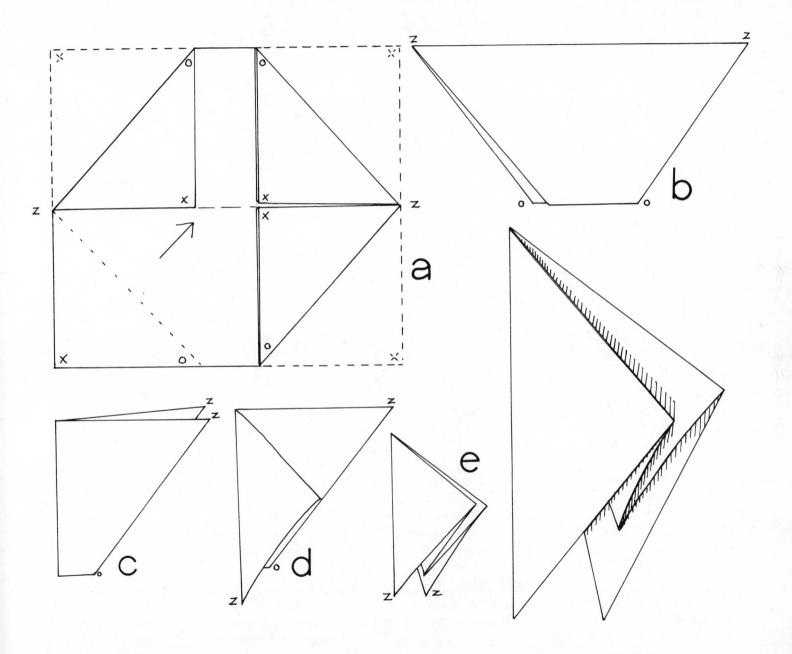

a

b

c

d

e

Confetti Balloons

One of the most important things you will be responsible for in getting ready for your party is decorating the house. Signs, streamers, and, of course, balloons should be scattered all around the house. When it's time to blow up the balloons, don't just fill them with hot air. Put a little something extra inside them. Have Mom buy some confetti. Before you blow up the balloons, put a little confetti in each. If you hang the balloons from the ceiling and you break them, it will rain confetti on your friends. (Remember to help Mom clean up all the spilled confetti after the party is over.)

Things You Need

colored felt-tipped markers   confetti
balloons   ribbon

Let's Begin

1. Put a little confetti in some of the balloons before you blow them up.
**2. Blow up the balloons and tie the end in a knot.
3. Use colored felt markers to draw designs on the balloons.
4. Tie a length of ribbon on the end of each balloon and hang them up.

Holidays
are fun

Holidays are fun

Life would be less fun if you didn't celebrate holidays. You would probably do the same things day after day, and school would be an extra month or two longer! Holidays are fun because, among other things, you learn all about history. Most holidays commemorate important historical events, or the birthdays of famous people. When you are in school, the week before a holiday is usually spent learning all about the special day. Although this is enjoyable, the best part of any holiday is not being in school but out of it. Holidays mean time off from your everyday "job."

To get you in the holiday spirit, eight projects have been designed for you. Whatever type of holiday you like, there will be at least one project having to do with it which you will enjoy making. After you finish making the first holiday project you will want to make all of them. This is good because you should be ready for as many holidays as you can.

A Very Special Valentine

It is said that Cupid delivers messages of love. If you have never seen Cupid—or don't know where to find him—don't worry (he is a very busy person on Valentine's Day). Why not send your own messages? You will make these very special valentines and send them to all your favorite people. They will love your love notes—and love the fact that you made them yourself.

Things You Need

1 sheet of tracing paper
pencil
scissors
paper paste
red, white, and black construction paper
crayons or colored felt-tipped markers

Let's Begin

1. Trace the inside and outside heart shapes separately from the book onto a sheet of tracing paper. Also trace the arrow.
2. Cut out the hearts and arrow tracings.
3. Trace the heart with the scalloped edge onto white construction paper.
4. Trace the plain heart onto red construction paper.
5. Trace the arrow onto black construction paper.
6. Cut out the hearts and the arrow.
7. Paste the red heart in the center of the white heart.
8. Cut two slits through both hearts like the ones shown on the smaller heart.
9. Slip the arrow through the two slits.
10. Write your message on the heart with crayons or colored felt-tipped markers.

Washington's Birthday Cherry Tree

George Washington is called the father of his country. He was America's first President. If you don't know what he did when he was President, you do know what he did when he was small. He chopped down his father's cherry tree. Not being a bad little boy, he told his father what he had done. He could not tell a lie. His father was proud of him for telling the truth. Now, don't you go outside and chop down a tree. Make one for your bedroom instead.

Things You Need

1 sheet of tracing paper
pencil
scissors
green and red construction paper
paper paste

Let's Begin

1. Trace the tree from the book onto a sheet of tracing paper.
2. Cut out the tracing.
3. Use the cutout to trace two trees on green construction paper.
4. Draw a slit on each tree. One tree has a slit going from the top to the middle of the tree. The other tree has a slit going from the bottom to the middle of the tree.
5. Cut out the trees and the slits.
6. Trace the leaf shape from the book onto tracing paper. Cut it out and, using it as a pattern, trace onto green construction paper. Do the same with the cherry shape, but trace it onto red construction paper. Make several of each shape.
7. Cut out the leaves and cherries and paste them to the sides of both trees. Be sure that the leaves and cherries are pasted away from the center slit.
8. Fit the slit on the bottom of one tree into the top slit of the other tree.
9. Push the two trees together so that the top and the bottom of the trees line up.
10. Stand the tree up.

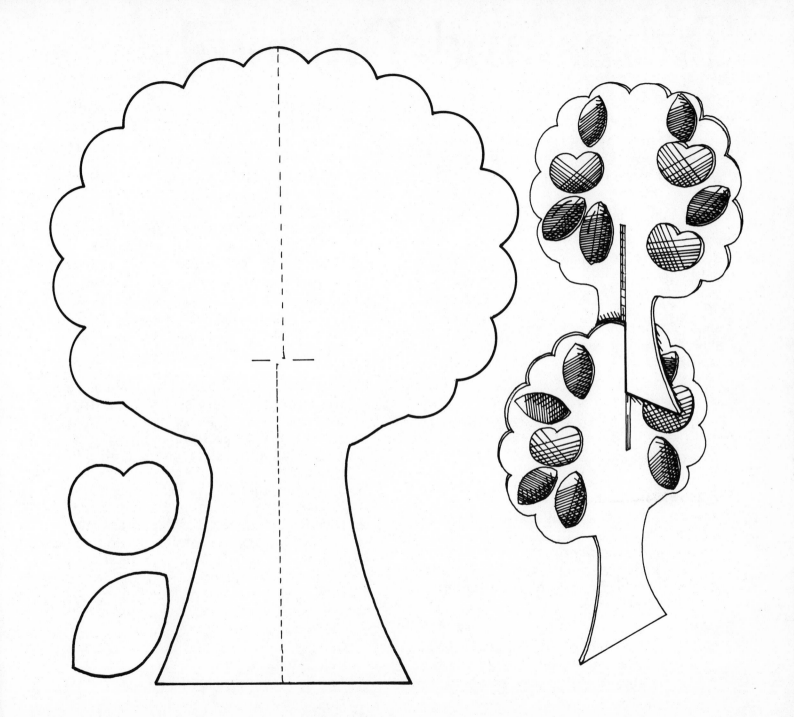

Tulips and Daffodils

Easter time is the flower season. This holiday arrives sometime during the spring when the flowers are starting to bloom. For a spring decoration, Easter-Egg Tulips and Daffodils will look as fresh as a bouquet of garden flowers.

Things You Need

blown eggs
indelible felt-tipped markers
drinking straws
green construction paper
liquid white glue
1 small clay or plastic flower pot
1 sheet of tracing paper
scissors
play clay
Easter grass
ribbon
pencil
pin or needle

Let's Begin

PRELIMINARIES

The tulips and daffodils are made from blown eggs. You will need at least two blown eggs for this project. To blow out an egg, see instructions in Ukrainian Pysanka Egg, page 200. Be sure to rinse the blown eggs; do not use soap.

TULIPS

**1. Make the hole on the wide end of a blown egg large enough to let a drinking straw fit through it. Push straw into egg.

2. Glue the straw to the eggshell. Let dry.

3. Hold the egg by the straw as you draw tulip petals on the shell with different colored felt-tipped markers.

4. Put a chunk of play clay into the bottom of a small flower pot.

5. Push the straws into the play clay.

6. Trace the tulip's leaf, Shape a, from the book onto a sheet of tracing paper.

7. Cut out the tracing and use it to trace leaves on green construction paper.

8. Cut out leaves and glue to the straws.

9. Fill the pot with Easter grass.

10. Tie a ribbon around the pot. Make a bow.

DAFFODILS

**1. Make a hole on the narrow end of a blown egg large enough to let a drinking straw fit through. Push straw into egg. Glue straw to egg and let dry.

2. Draw daffodil designs on eggshell with yellow and orange markers.

3. Trace the daffodil's petals, Shape b, from the book onto a sheet of tracing paper.

4. Cut out the tracing and use it as a pattern for cutting out petals on yellow construction paper. Punch a hole in the center of each petal.

5. Curl each petal upward.

6. Slip the petal on the straw and give it to the bottom of the egg.

7. Construct the pot of flowers the same way you did with the tulips.

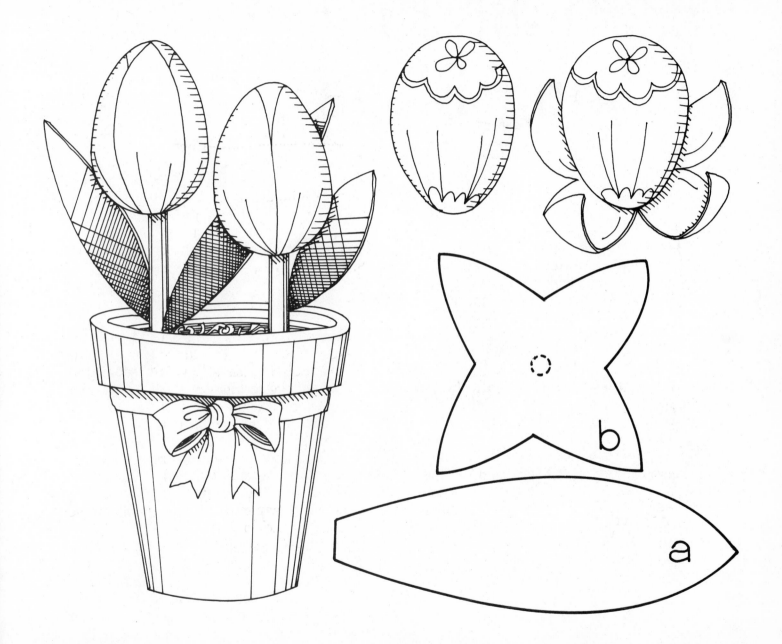

b

a

Fourth-of-July Hanging Flags

The Fourth of July is one of the most important holidays for the people of the United States of America. It was on July 4, 1776, that the Declaration of Independence was signed in Philadelphia. The United States became a free country. People were so very happy. Church bells rang and fireworks brightened the evening sky. The Liberty Bell was rung so hard that it cracked.

Today July 4th is celebrated with firework shows and programs about the meaning of the day. The most important thing to do is to show the Red, White, and Blue. In front of homes in your neighborhood, the American flag waves proudly. Why not bring some of the spirit of the celebration into your home with decorative hanging flags? They can be strung across a wall or hung, as patriotically as you like, in your window.

Things You Need

1 sheet of tracing paper
pencil
scissors
colored construction paper
tape
string
paper paste

Let's Begin

1. Trace the flag and the star separately from the book onto a sheet of tracing paper.
2. Cut out the tracings.
3. Use these cutouts to trace red, white, and blue flags and stars on construction paper.
4. Cut out the flags and stars.
5. Paste a star to each flag.
6. Fold the top of each flag along the dotted line (see illustration).
7. Place the folded top over a piece of string, Fig. a.
8. Tape the fold to the back of the flag, Fig. b.
9. Tape several flags onto the string, Fig. c.
10. Tape the string with the flags on a wall or across a window.

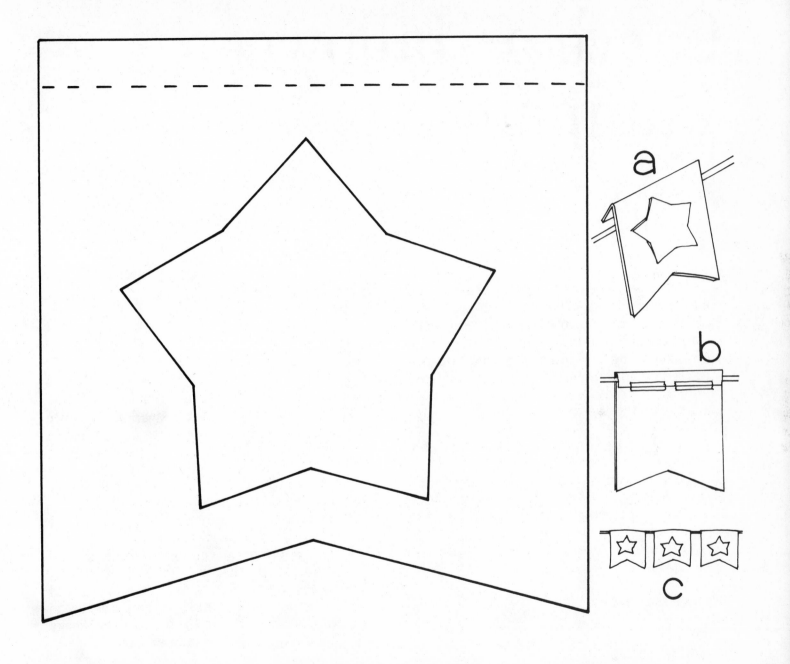

Carve a Halloween Pumpkin

Halloween is the day when witches, ghouls, goblins, and ghosts come out of hiding. It is fun dressing up in a costume and going trick-or-treating. If you are lucky, you can end up with a shopping bag of food, candy, and pennies. It is also fun to carve a big Halloween pumpkin. There is a song you should sing when you are carving the jack-o'-lantern:

First you get a pumpkin big, round, and fat.

Then you cut the top off, that makes the hat.

Then you cut the nose, the mouth and two eyes.

Making for the children a Halloween surprise.

Things You Need

1 pumpkin
knife and spoon
pie pan
birthday candles

Let's Begin

**1. First cut the top of the pumpkin, Fig. a. The top part is his hat.
  2. Use a spoon to scoop out all of the pulp and seeds. Save the seeds and put them in a pie pan, Fig. b.
**3. Use a knife to cut out the eyes, nose, and the mouth, Fig. c. Copy any of the shapes you see in the pumpkin illustrations.
  4. Poke a hole into the inside bottom of the pumpkin with a pencil.
  5. Put a birthday candle in the hole and light it. Put the "hat" on, Fig. d.
  6. Wash the pumpkin seeds you have saved with water. Sprinkle salt on the seeds and let them dry in the sun. In two weeks they will be delicious to eat.

Thanksgiving Placemats

A long time ago, the Pilgrims settled on the East Coast of America where they founded the Plymouth Colony. America was a strange country to them. Indians and wild animals lived in the forests and fields. Since the Pilgrims were the strangers in this new land, they had to learn how to live with the people and the creatures of America. Life was very hard at first, but the Pilgrims managed to endure. To celebrate this, and to express their thanks, they held one of the most famous dinners in history. It was the first Thanksgiving, and the colonists and Indians observed it together. Together they voiced their gratitude for all the things they had.

Today, Thanksgiving is the family holiday. If you don't have a turkey dinner in your own home, then you probably visit your aunts, uncles, or grandparents for dinner. The fun part of the day is watching the turkey being carved and eating all of the delicious food on the table. Now you can contribute to the Thanksgiving celebration by making turkey placemats for the table. Ask Mom how many people are visiting your home. Include yourself and your parents, too. Get started several weeks before Thanksgiving so your placemats will be ready when the guests arrive.

Things You Need

colored construction paper
1 sheet of tracing paper
crayons or colored felt-tipped markers
paper paste
scissors
pencil

Let's Begin

1. Cut out a circle larger than a dinner plate from orange construction paper.
2. Use the edge of a plate to draw a crescent shape on the paper circle, Fig. a. Use crayons or colored felt-tipped markers.
3. Draw a feather design on the crescent (see illustration).
4. Trace the turkey's-head shape and the small circle from the book onto a sheet of tracing paper.
5. Cut out the tracings.
6. Trace the head cutout onto brown construction paper and the circle onto red construction paper.
7. Cut out both shapes.
8. Paste the paper circle to the head (see illustration).
9. Paste the head to the body.
10. Put the dinner plates at your Thanksgiving dinner on the body part of your turkey placemats.

a

Chanukah Menorah

Chanukah is the Jewish Festival of Lights. It lasts eight days. During this holiday one candle is lit every day. Each day children receive gifts from their parents, and play games for pennies. The candles are placed in a menorah that is displayed in the house or by a window. You can celebrate Chanukah this year, and make your own menorah. It will be a lot of fun counting the days of this happy holiday.

Things You Need

colored construction paper
paper paste
drinking straws
scissors
pencil

Let's Begin

1. Fold a sheet of colored construction paper in four parts. Three parts should be exactly the same size and the fourth should be very small, Fig. a.
2. Fold the sheet into a triangle shape with the small fourth side tucked inside.
3. Paste the small side to the inside of the triangle.
4. Draw a menorah shape on construction paper big enough to fit on one side of the triangle. The menorah should have nine arms. (The ninth arm is for the candle used for lighting the other candles.)
5. Cut out the menorah and paste it to one side of the paper triangle.
6. Cut a small hole on the top fold of the triangle over each arm of the menorah.
7. Paste red paper flames to the top of nine drinking straws, Fig. b.
8. Place a straw candle into the middle hole.
9. Every night of the eight days of Chanukah add a straw candle to the menorah.

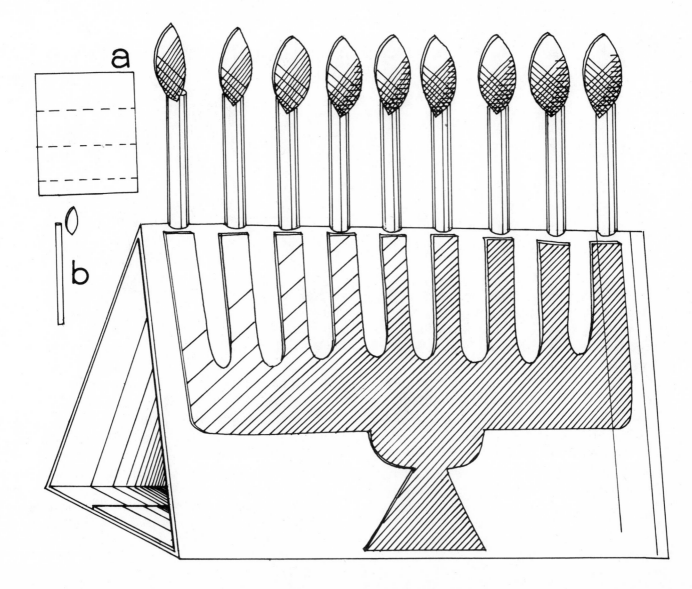

a

b

New Year's Eve Paper Hats

One of the noisest holidays of the year is New Year's Eve. It is important because it ushers in a new year. People look forward to doing new things. How do you celebrate this happy evening? If your parents let you stay up until midnight to see the coming of a new year, dress for the occasion. Make yourself a paper hat. If Mom and Dad don't have a hat, make extra ones for them. When the clock strikes twelve, welcome in the new year with a lot of noise. Blow horns, twirl rattlers, or beat a cooking pot with a large spoon.

Things You Need

colored construction paper
scissors
tape
stapler
ribbon

Let's Begin

1. Roll a sheet of colored construction paper to form a cone.
2. Tape the cone closed, Fig. a.
3. With scissors, trim the bottom edge of the cone to form an even circle, Fig. a.
4. Make a tassel for the top of the hat by cutting slits in a sheet of paper, Fig. b.
5. Roll the cut paper around itself to make a tassel and tape it in place on the top of the hat.
**6. Staple two pieces of ribbon onto both sides of the hat, Fig. c.

Santa
is coming
to town

Santa is coming to town

When Thanksgiving Day is over, Christmas is just around the corner. People start counting the days before the arrival of jolly old Saint Nick. They want to be sure they buy Christmas presents for everyone they love. The streets are decorated with colorful lights, red candles, and ringing bells. Stores decorate their windows and the latest toys are put on display. People somehow look a little different. They are smiling more because this is the merriest of all holidays. It is the spirit of Christmas that brings laughter and happiness to the world.

During the weeks before Christmas you probably look at the newest toys, games, and sports equipment. You want to be sure that Mom and Dad know exactly what you would like to have this year. If you are lucky enough, Santa may be visiting your neighborhood department store. He will want to know what everyone wants for Christmas. With a jolly "Ho, ho, ho," he will leave for the North Pole and get ready for the long sleigh ride on Christmas Eve. Mom and Dad may ask you what presents you want, but it's nice to believe that Santa delivers them to the house on December 25th.

Whatever you get, it is the Christmas spirit of love that makes the day really special. Everyone in your family is so happy during this holiday season. Everyone is busy preparing for the holiday, making food and decorating the house. This year you can make many pretty decorations for every corner of your home. There can never be enough Christmas decorations. Every room should ring out with holiday cheer. Make this the best Christmas you have ever had.

Santa Centerpiece

"Ho, ho, ho!" says Old Saint Nick. What person does not know these words? They are very popular at Christmas time. If there is no Santa Claus in your home, it is time to bring the jolly fat man into your dining room. Every time your family sits down for dinner, Santa Claus and the spirit of Christmas will be with you.

Things You Need

milk carton
colored construction paper
scissors
paper paste
cotton balls
liquid white glue
plastic or real poinsettias
kitchen cleanser

Let's Begin

1. Cut the top off a washed milk carton at the point where the rounded spout begins, Fig. a.

2. Cover the carton with a piece of pink construction paper and tape it together. Or paint the carton with pink poster paint that has kitchen cleanser added to it.
3. Paste a red paper strip around the top of the carton, Fig. b.
4. Glue cotton balls to the bottom half of the carton, Fig. b.
5. Trace the moustache and eyebrow shapes from the book onto a sheet of tracing paper.
6. Cut out the tracings.
7. Use the cutouts to trace two moustache shapes and two eyebrows on white paper.
8. Cut out the moustache and eyebrows.
9. Also cut out two black circle eyes, a red circle nose, two pink circle cheeks, and a red mouth, all from construction paper.
10. Paste the eyes, nose, cheeks, and mouth to the carton, Fig. c.
11. Paste on the eyebrows and the moustache last.
12. Put plastic poinsettias into the carton. Or you can use real flowers, first adding a little bit of water to the carton.

We Three Kings

It was the Three Kings who brought the gifts to the Christ Child during the first Christmas. Since that time the job of delivering gifts has been given to Santa Claus and his helpers all across the world. But you can still have the Three Kings visit your home on Christmas. Get out your scissors and paste to make sure of their prompt arrival.

Things You Need

colored construction paper
scissors
paper paste
tape
crayons or colored felt-tipped markers

Let's Begin

1. Roll a sheet of colored construction paper into a tube, Fig. a.
2. Tape the tube together, Fig. b.
3. Cut out two squares on opposite sides of the bottom of the tube, Fig. c. These cutouts form the legs. One of them should face you.
4. Make the face from a strip of pink, yellow, or brown construction paper pasted to the top of the tube.
5. Make the beards from strips of paper that have slits cut along their bottom edges.
6. Paste the beards under the strip of paper that forms the face, Fig. d.
7. Decorate the kings with cut paper shapes, and use crayons or colored felt-tipped markers for added designs.

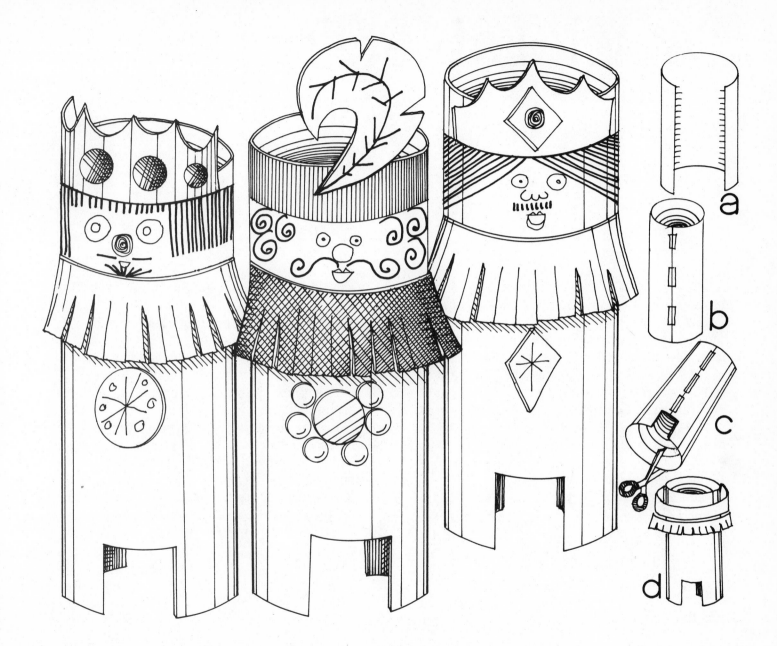

a

b

c

d

Tassel Table Tree

Nothing can take the place of a large Christmas tree standing tall in the living room. All of your family's favorite ornaments dangle from the branches. Although the tassel tree is not as tall and beautiful as a real Christmas tree, it will look pretty anywhere you want to put it. You might want a tassel tree in your room for the holidays.

Things You Need

1 large sheet of drawing paper
package of green crepe paper
scissors
paper paste
tape
yellow paper or gold stick-on stars
cardboard tube from a roll of paper towels

Let's Begin

1. Cut the drawing paper in a half-circle. It should be two times longer than it is wide, Fig. a.
2. Roll the half-circle into a cone, Fig. b.
3. Tape the cone together.
4. If the bottom of the cone does not form an even circle, trim it with your scissors.
5. Cut a package of green crepe paper into strips, Fig. c.
6. Cut slits in each strip halfway up, Fig. d.
7. Open the strips.
8. Paste a fringed strip to the cone at the bottom edge, Fig. e.
9. Keep gluing strips onto the cone, overlapping rows. Cover the entire cone.
10. Paste yellow construction paper stars or gold stick-on stars to the tree.
11. Stand the tree on a table. If it is small enough, stand the tree on a paper-towel tube, Fig. e.

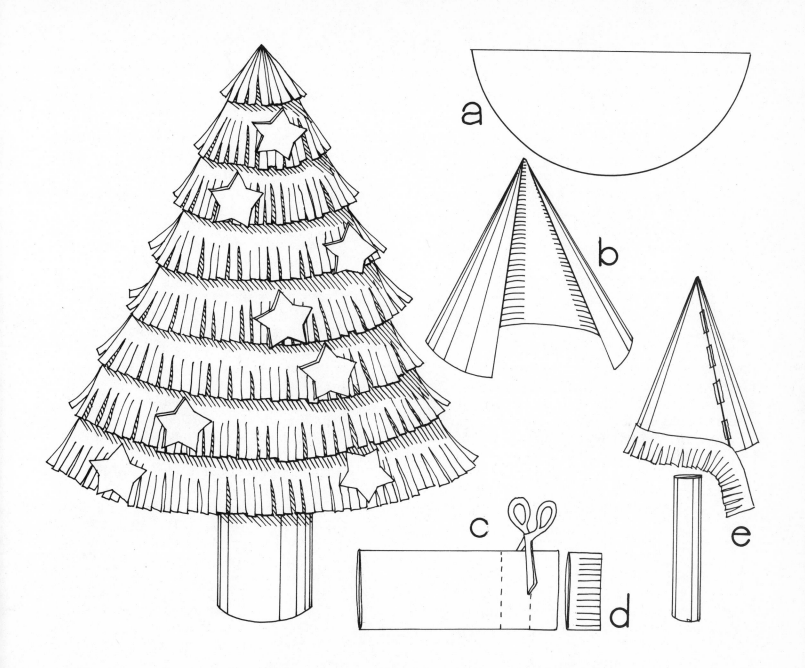

a

b

c

d

e

Mr. Snow the Snowman

Wintertime means snow and building snowmen and snowwomen. After you make one, you often want to bring it indoors with you. The problem is that it will melt in a few hours. Here is one snowman that won't turn to a watery puddle. Mr. Snow the Snowman will stay as crisp as new fallen snow all during the holiday season. Find him a place in your home this Christmas.

Things You Need

oatmeal or salt box
3-inch foam ball
4 one-inch foam balls
colored construction paper
1 sheet of tracing paper
white poster paint
drinking straw
liquid white glue
small length of scrap fabric
knife
scissors

Let's Begin

1. Trace the hat and broom shapes from the book onto a sheet of tracing paper.

2. Cut out the tracings.
3. Use the cutouts to trace a hat on black construction paper and the broom on yellow construction paper.
4. Cut out the hat and broom.
5. To make Mr. Snow, first paint a salt or oatmeal box with white poster paint, or wrap in white paper and tape.
**6. Cut a little slice from each foam ball with a knife, Fig. a. The flat side of the foam balls is the side that will be glued to the box.
7. Glue the large ball to the top of the box for a head.
8. Glue two of the small balls to the box near the top for the arms.
9. Cut two more slices from the remaining small balls opposite the first slices. The bottom slices help Mr. Snow to stand.
10. Glue the balls to the bottom of the box on opposite sides.
11. Glue the head of the broom to a drinking straw.
12. Glue the drinking straw to one of Mr. Snow's hands.
13. Make Mr. Snow's eyes, nose, mouth, and buttons from construction-paper circles and glue them on.
14. Tie a piece of scrap fabric around Mr. Snow's neck.

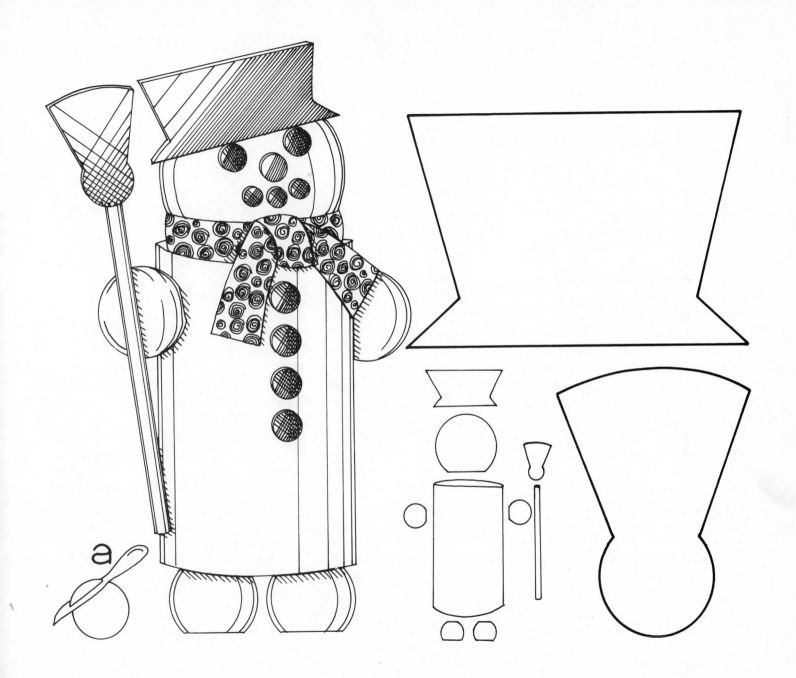

a

Holly Wreath

During the Christmas season your entire home is dressed in holiday attire. One of the first things your friends and relatives see when they come to your home is the wreath on your door. Wreaths come in all sizes and shapes. They can be made from almost anything. The most popular wreath is made from branches of pine with a big red ribbon tied to the bottom in a bow. If your door already has a wreath, then why not make one for the door to your room? It will provide a Christmas welcome for your friends when they come to visit you.

Things You Need

green and red construction paper
1 sheet of tracing paper
pencil
scissors
1 large sheet of cardboard or drawing paper
large plate
paper paste

Let's Begin

1. Trace around the rim of a large plate onto a large sheet of cardboard or drawing paper.
2. Using a smaller plate, trace a smaller circle shape in the center of the large one, Fig. a.
3. Cut out the outer circle first, then the inside circle, Fig. b.
4. Trace the leaf shape from the book onto a sheet of tracing paper.
5. Cut out the tracing.
6. Use the cutout to trace many leaves on green construction paper.
7. Cut out the leaves.
8. Cut out circles from red construction paper. (You can trace around a quarter for perfect circles.)
9. Paste the first leaf on the cardboard circle, Fig. c.
10. Paste the second leaf a little away from the first, overlapping it slightly, Fig. d.
11. Cover the wreath with leaves pasted slightly on top of each other.
12. Paste the red circles on the leaves for holly berries.
13. Use string to hang in a window or on a door.

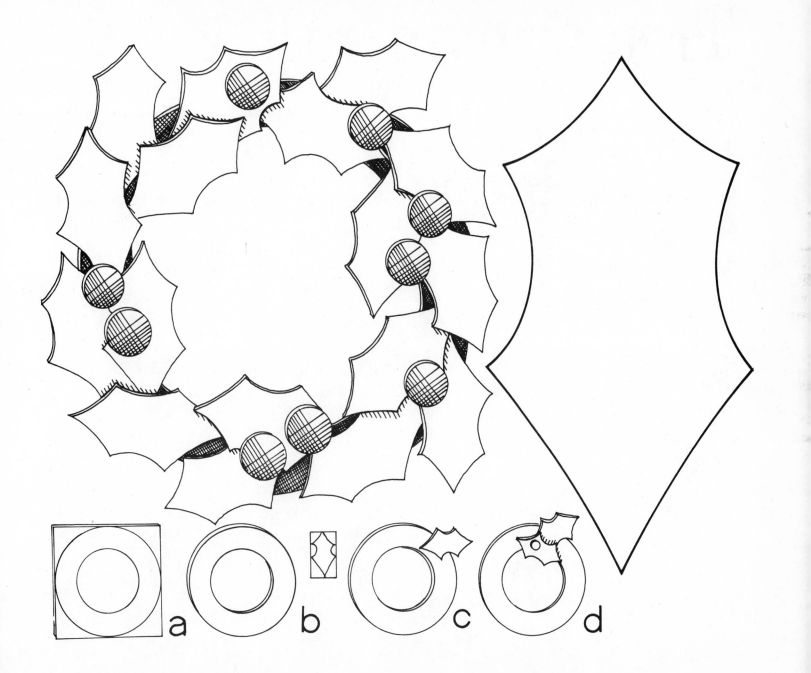

a   b   c   d

Tree Ornaments

Here are some more ornaments you can make for your Christmas tree. The last set of ornaments were made from paper. Now you are going to use other materials found around your home. Paper chains, bells, silver tassels, and candy cups will add the finishing touch to your already pretty tree. Be sure to find special places for these constructed ornaments.

Things You Need

aluminum foil
scissors
stapler
paper cone cups
pipe cleaners
kitchen cleanser
small Christmas balls
wrapped hard candy
colored construction paper
poster paints
paper paste

Let's Begin

SILVER TASSELS
1. Cut slits in a sheet of aluminum foil, Fig. a.
2. Roll the foil around itself in a tight circle, Fig. b.
3. Staple the foil together at the top.

4. Glue or staple a piece of paper or ribbon to the top of the tassel for hanging (see illustration).

BELLS
1. Paint paper cone cups with poster paints. If the paint won't stick to the cups, add a bit of cleanser to it.
2. Attach one end of a pipe cleaner to the wire loop of a small Christmas ball.
3. Push the other end through the top of the cone.
4. Twist the pipe cleaner into a small loop.
5. Tie a piece of string through the top loop.

CANDY CUPS
1. Paint paper cups with poster paints.
2. Staple a paper strip to both sides of the cup for a handle.
3. Fill with wrapped candy, and hang on a branch.

PAPER CHAINS
1. Cut construction-paper strips as long and as wide as the three links in the illustration.
2. Bend one strip into a circle and paste the ends together, Figs. c and d.
3. Put a second strip of paper into the circle and bend this strip into a circle, Figs. e, f, g. Paste the ends of this loop together.
4. Continue forming and pasting loops until you make a long chain.

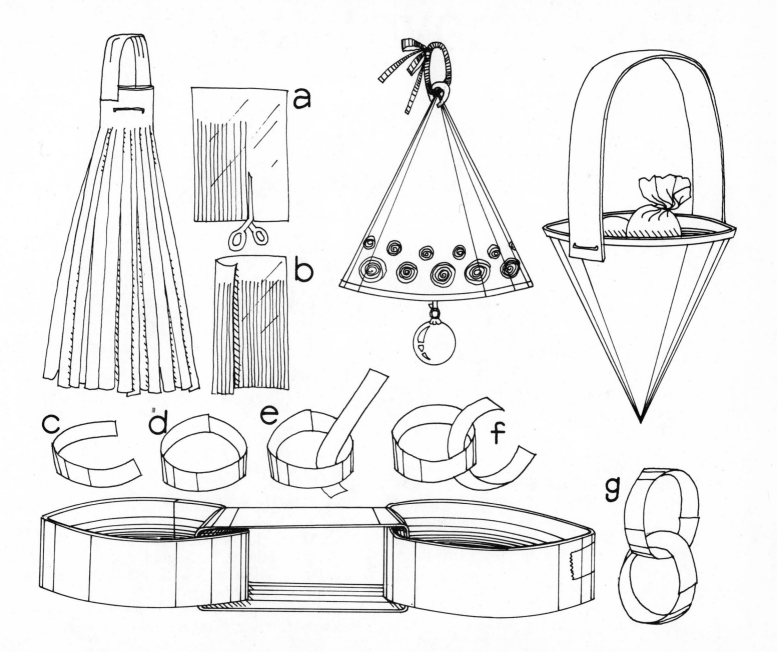

a

b

c d e f

g

Paper Snowflakes

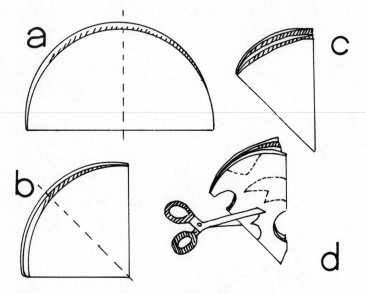

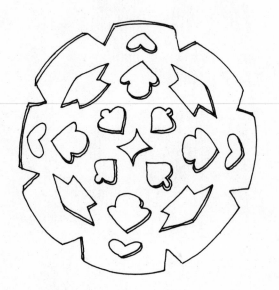

This year make your home look really wintery. Hang snowflakes in every room and in every window. When Old Saint Nick stops at your home, he will feel as if he is back at the North Pole. You might want to leave a few cookies or a piece of pie for this weary traveler.

Things You Need

typewriter or white drawing paper
scissors

Let's Begin

1. Cut white paper circles.
2. Fold the circles in half, Fig. a.
3. Fold the circles in half again, Fig. b.
4. Fold the circles in half again, Fig. c.
5. Cut out different shapes along the sides and the top of the folded circles, Fig. d.
6. Open the circles. You will never make two snowflakes exactly alike.

Puppets are almost people

Puppets are almost people

Many of your best play friends are puppets. They are the closest thing to real people because they look and act as if they were alive. You can move their hands, legs, feet, mouths, and heads. By changing your voice, you can make them sound like different characters. They provide hours of fun for yourself and for your friends when they come to your home.

There was one famous puppet that became a real person. His name was Pinocchio. A woodcarver called Gepetto created him because he was lonely. Pinocchio was made from wood, but the day after he was created he began to talk. Gepetto was surprised but very happy. At last he had a talking friend. But Pinocchio was too curious about the world. He often ran away from Gepetto and would not come back for days. He even starred in a puppet show. Everyone was amazed to see a puppet without strings.

Pinocchio set out in search of new things. He met all kinds of people. He got in trouble several times. Finally he found himself in a really terrible situation. He became friends with a hooky player named Lamp Wick. They went to the Lands of Fun and Games when they should have been in school. It turned out not to be fun at all. Pinocchio finally escaped

but, in doing so, he landed in the ocean. He was swallowed by Monstro the Whale. Inside the whale's stomach he found Gepetto, who had been swallowed while searching for his little wooden puppet. They both managed to escape and ride to the shore on a tuna fish. Pinocchio saved Gepetto.

Gepetto and Pinocchio were finally together. They went home after their long search for each other. The next morning, when Pinocchio opened his eyes, he noticed something different. He was no longer a puppet. He was a real little boy. His good deed had made his wish to be real come true. Pinocchio and Gepetto lived happily for many years.

If you like the story of Pinocchio and enjoy playing with puppets, you are in for a treat. In this chapter you will make a puppet theater, scenery, puppets, tickets, and programs. A happy play, *Santina and the Whispering Willow*, is included. There is even a snack bar to sell tasty things to eat during the intermission. It is going to take many days, even weeks, before you finish all of the necessary things for a puppet show. But when you do, you will be the director of the best puppet theater in your neighborhood.

A Play–Santina and the Whispering Willow

Characters

NARRATOR
SANTINA
KING ANTHONY
PRINCE OF SIAM
PRINCE OF IRAN
PRINCE NOEL OF FRANCE
LITTLE BOY

ACT I

Scene: *The palace garden. A weeping willow tree is at the left of the stage.*

Curtain is closed throughout first speech

NARRATOR (*Spoken from backstage*)

In olden times, in the kingdom of Serene,
Lived the princess, Santina,
The fairest to be seen—
The lovely daughter of the great King
  Anthony.

Santina had a peacock with snow-white
  down
And a red marble throne,
And a bright golden crown.
She had a different dress for each day of
  the year.

In the palace garden stood an old willow
  tree.
Much closer to Santina than anything
  could be.

Open curtain

(*Enter* SANTINA *from the right side of the stage*)

SANTINA (*Looking at the willow tree*)
Oh dear willow, I will never leave thee.

(*Enter* KING ANTHONY. *He speaks from behind* SANTINA)

KING ANTHONY (*Softly*)
Oh lovely Daughter by the willow tree,
Turn your pretty face and look at me.

SANTINA (*Turns and looks at her father. She is in a daze*)
Dearest Father, are you speaking to me?

KING ANTHONY
An order has been sent to princes of the
  land.
A contest will soon be held to win your lovely
  hand.
The winner will have my kingdom.

SANTINA (*Turns away from her father and*

298

stares at the willow tree)
I don't like these words you are saying.
By my willow tree I want to be staying.

KING ANTHONY (*In an angry voice*)
And the winner will have my kingdom.

SANTINA (*Runs to the willow tree and puts
her arms around it*)

Soon I will have to select a bridegroom.
Oh, my wise old tree,
How lovely is your bloom.
Please spread your weeping branches and
　　comfort me.

Curtain

ACT II

Scene: KING ANTHONY'S *chamber. The king is
sitting at the right of the stage.* PRINCESS
SANTINA *is sitting in the middle of the stage.*

Open Curtain

NARRATOR (*Spoken from backstage*)
　It is one week later in the early morning
　Came the young Prince of Siam
　With his hands bearing
　Precious jewels from the Orient land.

(THE PRINCE OF SIAM *enters from the left.
He moves to the center of the stage and bows
in front of* SANTINA. *He holds out his hands
full of jewels*)

PRINCE OF SIAM
　Diamonds, rubies, and a silver pearl ring
　Are all yours, my sweet princess.
　Take these valuable gifts I bring.
　Your love is what I desire.

SANTINA (*Looking at the* PRINCE)
　Kind prince, your fine jewels do not
　Impress me,
　And you are much too tall,
　So I reject thee.

PRINCE OF SIAM (*With his head facing the
　　　　　　floor*)
　Since it is me you do not want, I will leave.

(PRINCE OF SIAM *exits from the right*)

NARRATOR (*Spoken from backstage*)
　The second suitor, very tall and bright,
　Was a prince from Iran,
　A stately, handsome knight.

(THE PRINCE OF IRAN *enters from the left.
He moves to the center of the stage and bows
in front of* SANTINA)

Continued on next page

PRINCE OF IRAN (*Holding his hands apart*)
    I bring no jewels, only what you see.
    My handsome face is my gift to thee.
    I am sure that I will please.

SANTINA (*Feeling sorry for the prince*)
    It is a fact that you are quite handsome,
    But twiddling your thumbs
    Will be very hard for you to overcome.
    Oh handsomest of knights, you just won't do.

(PRINCE OF IRAN *exits from the right*)

KING ANTHONY (*Moves to* SANTINA)
    Such silly things does my daughter reject.
    Why couldn't you try to be a little less
      select?

SANTINA
    Oh kindest father, you will never get an
      heir to your kingdom this way.

Curtain

ACT III

Scene: *Outside the palace gates. On a dirt road that leads to Serene.*

Open Curtain

NARRATOR (*Spoken from backstage*)

In the passing of time the nineteenth prince
Could not persuade,
Nor could he convince
The loyal Santina that he might win her
    love.

Now on the highway that leads to Serene
Walks Prince Noel of France,
Firstborn of a queen.

PRINCE NOEL
    Little boy, why does Santina turn so many
      away?

LITTLE BOY
    It is true that I'm a boy of five,
    But I am sure the secret
    Is easy to derive.
    It is the willow in her garden she will
      not leave.

PRINCE NOEL (*Shaking the* LITTLE BOY's *hand*)
    Thank you, you have told me very much.
    I must be traveling so I may touch
    The hand of beautiful Santina.

LITTLE BOY
    Many handsome princes passed this way.
    All brought gifts and promises,
    But none did stay
    To rule the kingdom of Serene.
    (*Exit* LITTLE BOY *from the left*)

PRINCE NOEL (*To himself*)
The mystery now has become very clear.
What the little boy has told me
Has given me an idea.
To the palace I must travel very quickly.

Curtain

(INTERMISSION)

ACT IV

Scene: *The palace garden.* SANTINA *is by the weeping willow tree.*

Open Curtain

(*During the following speech* PRINCE NOEL *searches for the willow tree. When he finds the tree he hides behind it.*)

NARRATOR (*Spoken from backstage*)
In the garden Prince Noel searched
        throughout,
            until he found the willow
            with its branches all about.
He climbed the old tree to the highest
        branch.

He listened from his branch so high
            and from inside the palace walls
            he heard a sad cry.
Santina rejected the twentieth prince.

(SANTINA *walks onstage and to the willow tree*)

SANTINA (*Very happy*)
Number twenty has heard my answer.
He pretended to be a prince
But he was only a dancer.
Dear willow, I am still as free as you.

PRINCE NOEL (*From behind the tree*)
Santina my dear, I am so fond of you.
You have such deep love
And remained so true.
Your kindness is music to my heart.

SANTINA (*Very surprised. Looks up at the tree*)
You startle me, but could this really be
That here I stand before you
Speaking words with my tree?
Then my love for you has been worthwhile.

PRINCE NOEL
Your love for me has been appreciated.
I am grateful for the young men
You have eliminated.
I am sleepy now, come back in the morning.

SANTINA
Oh speak no more, for I will go.
In the morning when I awake,
I will know
That the morning sun will lead me to you.

301   *Continued on next page*

(*Exit* SANTINA *from the right*)

PRINCE NOEL (*Jumps down from the tree to the stage*)
It worked! She really thinks it has been
The tree
Who has been talking to her,
But it was really me.
Oh willow, the first part of my plan is done.

Curtain

ACT V

Scene: *It is the following day. The sun is shining brightly (pin a paper sun to the back curtain).* SANTINA *is by the willow tree in the palace garden.*

Open Curtain

NARRATOR (*Spoken from backstage*)
In the morning of the very next day
The willow and Santina
Had many things to say.
He whispered softly to her of faraway
    places.

SANTINA (*Looking at the tree*)
The rays of the sun have brought me to your
Branches.
The night went by so fast
That there weren't any chances
To say how much I love you.

PRINCE NOEL (*From behind the tree*)
I remember a land with dragons all around.

SANTINA (*Very excited*)
Hurry, tell me more interesting things.

PRINCE NOEL
Please don't interrupt with the sound your
    tired voice is making.

SANTINA
I have lived behind these palace walls,
But over it I cannot see,
And you are so very tall.
Your stories of dragons, jesters, and snow-
    white doves must be true.

PRINCE NOEL
I love you, my princess, but I am sad of
Heart.
Oh lovely Santina,
We will have to part.
I'm dying of old age and to heaven I must go.

SANTINA (*Sniffling*)
Speak not these words, my faithful
    whispering tree.
You are the prince of my choosing.
Can't you see that I love thee?
If you must go, then I will follow you.

(PRINCE NOEL *jumps from behind the tree in front of* SANTINA)

NARRATOR (*Spoken from backstage*)
At first Santina was as angry as can be,
Knowing that this young stranger
Was the voice of her favorite tree.
Then she knew that it was the Prince she
    really loved.

SANTINA (*Looking at* PRINCE NOEL)
So it was a prince who spoke of beautiful
Places,
Not my dearest willow tree,
Whom no prince replaces.
The willow tree will always be with me.

PRINCE NOEL (*Taking her hand*)
It is you I want to live with forever,
And with your willow tree.
You and I will never,
Never leave each other until the sun shines
No more.

(SANTINA *and* PRINCE NOEL *walk offstage*
while THE NARRATOR *speaks.*)

NARRATOR (*Spoken from backstage*)
And shortly after, Serene was to see
The loveliest of weddings
Beneath the willow tree.
They soon lived in a palace of their own.

It took twenty-nine men to move the willow
    tree.
And there it is standing
In its new home by the sea,
As another small Santina takes the willow
    to her heart.

And they did indeed live happily ever after.

Curtain

THE END

Puppet Theater

When your parents take you to the movies you go to a theater to see the show. If you have never seen a play at school or somewhere else, the actors perform on stage. If you want to put on a puppet show, then you will need your own theater or stage. This stage is very easy to make. All you need is a large cardboard carton and you can change your bedroom into a real performing theater.

Things You Need

large cardboard carton
knife or scissors
scrap fabric
string
needle and thread
poster paints
paintbrush
pencil
ruler

Let's Begin

**1. Cut away the top of the carton, Fig. a.
2. Draw a stage opening on the front of the carton with a pencil. It should be shaped like a square with rounded corners on top, Fig. b.
**3. Cut out the stage opening, Fig. b.
4. Measure with a ruler and note the distance from the top of the carton to the top of the stage opening.
5. Draw a line around the other three sides of the box that is as far from the top as the distance you measured, Fig. c.
6. Draw two x's at the front right- and left-hand edges of the box which are even with the top of the stage opening, Fig. c. Draw a line from the x points on both sides of the theater to opposite bottom corner, z.
**7. Cut away the triangular areas formed by the lines on both sides of the box, blackened area in Fig. c.
**8. Cut away the back of the carton up to the drawn line, blackened area in Fig. d. The remaining top part of the carton on the back and sides is called the curtain bar.
9. Push out and forward the two triangle wings on the sides, Fig. d.
**10. Cut away the bottom of the carton, Fig. e.
11. Place the theater on the back edge of a table with the wings facing front onto the table. Tape it to the table on the inside of the front and on the back wings, Figs. g and h.

304

(continued on page 306)

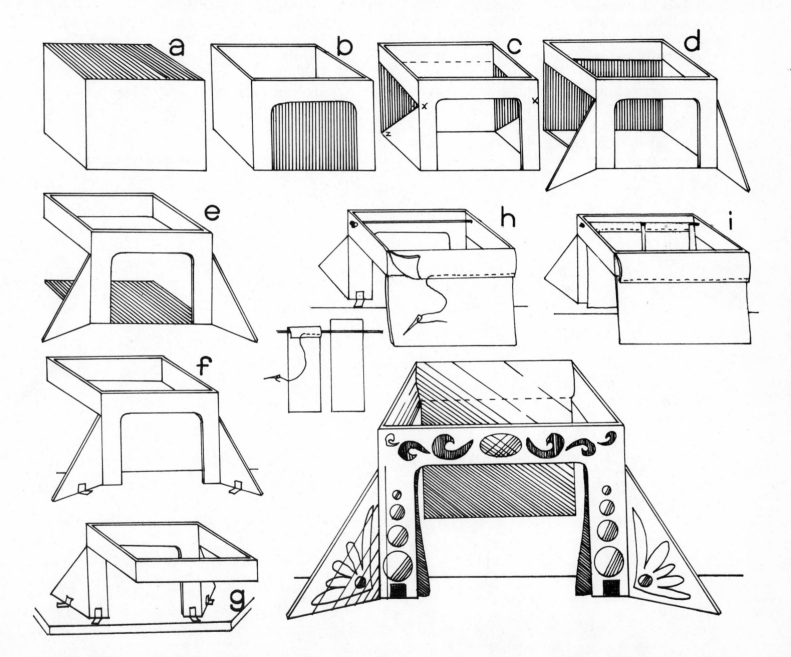

a   b   c   d   e   f   g   h   i

12. Cut a back curtain from the scrap fabric to fit the width of the back curtain bar. Add extra to the length of the curtain so that it can be wrapped around the curtain bar. Fold the curtain over the curtain bar and sew it as shown in Fig. h.
13. Make the front curtain from two pieces of fabric wide enough to cover the stage opening when "closed."
14. Punch a hole through each side of the theater a little bit back from the front. Run a cord through the holes and knot, Fig. h.
15. Fold the two front curtains over the cord and sew as shown, Figs. h and i.
16. Paint designs on the theater with poster paints. Work puppets from below back of table, sticking hands up through the open bottom of the theater.

Santina's Willow Tree

Weeping willow trees are very pretty because their branches seem to be kissing the ground. They look like huge green umbrellas, or giants with green hair. The willow is very important in this play. It is Santina's only love. She is very happy when she is in the palace garden by the willow tree. Although the tree can't talk, the prince in the tree talks as if he were the willow. Santina believes the tree is really talking. The willow tree is one of the important objects on your stage. Make it as pretty as you can.

Things You Need

cardboard tube from bathroom-tissue rolls
drinking straws
string
green construction paper
tracing paper
pencil
scissors
poster paints
paintbrush
colored felt-tipped markers
play clay

Let's Begin

1. Tie a handful of straws together close to the bottom, Fig. a.
2. Spread out the straws like a fan.
3. Paint the tube with brown poster paint.
4. Draw a bark design on the tube with a dark colored felt-tipped marker.
5. To put the tree together, push the straws into the top of the tube trunk. Wedge a piece of play clay into the bottom of the tube, Fig. b.
6. You can either cut out your own leaves or trace the leaf shape from the book. If you are going to trace the shape, first trace it onto tracing paper.
7. Cut out the tracing and use it as a pattern to trace many leaves onto green construction paper. Cut out leaves.
8. Glue the leaves to the straw branches.

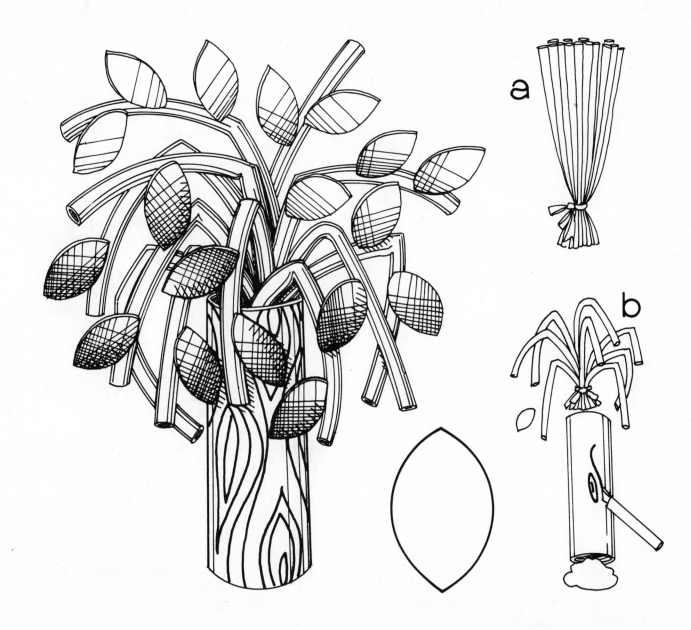

a

b

Ball-and-Pencil Puppets

Now that you have your stage and the weeping willow tree, it is time to make the principal characters. Santina, King Anthony, and Prince Noel of France are your three main characters. There are two other princes: the Prince of Siam and the Prince of Iran. When you make these two other princes, make sure their faces and clothing are different from those of the other characters. There is also a Little Boy who is very important in the story. Make a basic puppet shape and draw on a little boy's face. The puppets are made from pencils, ping-pong balls, and construction paper.

Things You Need

ping-pong balls or foam balls
pencils
colored construction paper
scrap fabric
needle and thread
colored yarn
liquid white glue
crayons or colored felt-tipped markers

Let's Begin

1. The puppet skirts should be cut wide enough to go around your hand with plenty of room to spare. They should be long enough to pass beyond your wrist. To make a skirt, first cut a sufficiently large piece of scrap fabric which is fairly rectangular.

2. Fold the fabric in half along the length, Fig. a.

**3. Thread a needle and knot the thread.

4. Sew the two sides of the fabric together a little in from the edges, Fig. a.

5. Sew the last stitch several times before you cut the thread.

6. Turn the skirt inside out.

**7. Thread the needle again.

8. This time sew a loose stitch around the top of the skirt a little down from the top edge, Fig. b. Do not cut the thread when finished.

9. To make the puppet, punch a sharp pencil into a ping-pong ball or a foam ball.

10. Add a dab of glue under the ball if it does not fit tightly on the pencil.

11. Push the pencil into the top of the skirt, Fig. c.

12. Pull the needle and thread tightly to trap the pencil, just under the ball.

13. Go over the last stitch several times before you cut the thread.

14. Glue on yarn hair and paper crowns, and draw faces with crayons or colored felt-tipped markers.

15. Add ribbon or yarn around the neck. Santina has beads around her neck.

16. NOTE: The Prince of Siam, the Prince of Iran and the Little Boy are made from the same puppet shapes as Prince Noel but only in different colors and with different faces.

a

b

c

Soap-Bottle Puppets

Your puppet show will be such a great success that you will have to perform it many, many times. What you will need for new performances is a new cast of actors. The same characters will be played by a different cast of puppets. You probably thought that empty plastic soap bottles should be thrown in the garbage. Save as many of these soap bottles as you can. They make wonderful hand puppets. With your finger in the bottle's spout, you can make a character do many things. Now you have a reason for helping Mom with the dishes. She will help you collect as many as you need.

Things You Need

small plastic soap bottles (the kind that
   dishwashing liquid comes in)
scrap fabric
needle and thread
ribbon and fringe
indelible felt-tipped markers

liquid white glue

Let's Begin

1. Make the puppet heads from plastic soap bottles with the opening turned upside down. Draw faces and hair on the bottles with indelible felt-tipped markers.
2. Glue yellow paper crowns on top of the face.
3. Make the skirt the same way as you did in the Ball-and-Pencil Puppets, page 310.
4. Pull the skirt around the indented part of the bottle. (See the dotted line in the King Anthony Puppet illustration.)
5. Cover the pulled stitches with bits of ribbon and fringe.
6. To work the puppets, put your finger into the opening of the bottle under the skirt.
7. NOTE: The Prince of Siam, the Prince of Iran, and the Little Boy are the same puppet shapes as Prince Noel but only in different colors and with different faces.

312

Paper-Bag Puppets

You probably thought that paper bags were used only for carrying groceries home from the supermarket, or for carrying your lunch to school. They make wonderful hand puppets, too. Your artistic creativity will be seen when these puppets are performing on stage. You can draw the entire face and body of paper-bag puppets. They are soft enough to bend and do all kinds of things, almost like the sock puppets. Mom will save all of her smaller grocery bags for you. Be sure to help her do the shopping, and carry some of the bags for her before you use them.

Things You Need

small brown paper bags

colored construction paper
crayons or colored felt-tipped markers
paper paste

Let's Begin

1. Draw King Anthony, Santina, Prince Noel, the Prince of Siam, the Prince of Iran, and the Little Boy, each on one side of a bag. (Only Santina, King Anthony, and Prince Noel are shown in the illustration.)
2. Paste crowns cut from yellow construction paper to the top of each bag puppet.
3. To work the puppets, put your hand inside the bags.

Programs and Invitations

Now that the scenery, theater, and puppets are made, it is time to send out invitations for your performance. The invitation is a ticket that your guests have to present to you before the show begins. After they have handed you their ticket, give them a program that lists the characters and the person who is speaking for each character. Once all the tickets have been collected, let the show begin. Dim the lights and open the curtain on the first performance of *Santina and the Whispering Willow*.

Things You Need

colored construction paper
scissors
crayons or colored felt-tipped markers

Let's Begin

1. The program tells your guests all about the play they are about to see. The names shown on the program in the book are only examples. You will write in the correct names of the people who will be speaking for the puppets. Copy the program information on sheets of colored construction paper.
2. Hand one to each guest as he arrives.
3. The invitations should be given to each invited guest a few days before the puppet show. Copy the invitation from the book as many times as necessary on colored construction paper. Put in the appropriate date, time, and name.
4. Ask each guest to bring his invitation with him on the day of the puppet show.
5. Rip off the part of the invitation that says Admit 1 Person before letting the guest take his seat.

Santina
and
the Whispering Willow

○

Voice of Santina - Mary

Voice of King Anthony
and Narrator - Greg

Voice of Prince Noel
boy and other princes - Mark

○

Play in 5 acts

Intermission after the
third act

○

Scenery, Puppets, Stage
Mary & Mark Smith

Refreshments - Mrs. Smith

Santina
and the Whispering Willow

○○○

Sat. - August 21, 19__
2:00 — 3:00

at Mary and Mark Smith's
Basement

- - - - - - - - - - - - - - - - - -

ADMIT
1
PERSON

Snack Bar

Your puppet show has five acts. When you see a play at a theater there is an intermission after each act. This is so that the actors can have a little rest before the next act, and the audience can stretch and have something to eat or drink. Your intermission will come after the third act. Notice of the intermission will be written on the programs. Your guests will want a snack by the time the third act is over. Fill your snack bar with wrapped hard candy and a pitcher of fruit drink. Popcorn is also a good thing to have. Don't make the intermission too long. Your guests will be waiting to see what will happen to Santina and the willow.

Things You Need

large cardboard carton
scissors
tape
ruler
colored construction paper
paper paste
bowl of popcorn
candy
contact paper
paper cups
pitcher of juice or lemonade

Let's Begin

1. Tape the open end of a cardboard carton closed, Fig. a.
2. Turn the box upside down so that the taped end is on the bottom.
**3. Cut away one of the box's sides, Fig. a.
4. With a ruler, measure the depth of the inside of the box, Fig. c.
5. Measure the same depth on the cardboard side you removed, and draw a cutting line across the width.
**6. Cut away the extra cardboard from this side, Fig. b.
7. Fit this piece of cardboard into the box for a shelf.
8. Tape the shelf to the inside of the box.
9. Decorate the front of the box with a paper sign and arrows pointing to where the line should form.
10. Paste some paper decorations to the front of the box and write your Mom's name or your name on it. You might ask Mom for some contact paper to stick to the top of the snack bar. In case some juice is spilled, all you need is a wet sponge to wipe the top of the snack bar clean and dry. Put goodies on the shelf and you're in business!

318

a

b

c

Mrs. Smith's Snack Bar

Good-bye

Congratulations! You have come to the end of *Sticks & Stones & Ice Cream Cones*. It wasn't easy getting to this page. You spent many happy hours making these fun-filled crafts. There were probably many times when you thought you would never finish a project. If you tried your very best and completed the projects you liked the best, then you deserve an award. Consider yourself the proud recipient of the Certificate of Achievement you see in the book, and sign your name in the proper place. Remember, if you like to use your hands and make things, this book can be enjoyed over and over again.

Certificate of Achievement

✳✳✳✳✳

AWARDED TO

_____

Phyllis Fiarotta ♥
AUTHORIZED SIGNATURE